When The Lost Get Found

Confronting the Prodigal in You and Me

walter spires

When the Lost Get Found

Trilogy Christian Publishers A Wholly Owned Subsidiary of Trinity Broadcasting Network

2442 Michelle Drive Tustin, CA 92780

Edited by Dave Boehi

Cover design by Daniel Shifflet
Photography by Elijah Hiett
Manufactured in the United States of America
10 9 8 7 6 5 4 3 2 1
Library of Congress Cataloging-in-Publication Data is available.
ISBN: 978-1-63769-742-9
E-ISBN: 978-1-63769-743-6

Dedication

This book is dedicated to two men, both Home with the Lord, who had tremendous influence in and on my life: Dane Miller and Gus Sideris.

Dane and I met during my collegiate years. I grew to love him as an older brother. He was also a great friend and advisor. Dane later extended two invitations to me that helped shape and change my life professionally and, more importantly, spiritually.

Dane invited me to join him and a few others to begin a new orthopedic venture. It was a great opportunity, hard work, and a lot of fun. I was a single young man from the South, now in a small midwestern town in which I knew no one but Dane. His family, as well as the other three who were part of that venture, made me feel part of theirs during those early years.

While Dane's first invitation helped shape my life professionally, the second had a more personal, profound, and eternal impact. He invited me to go to church with his family. It was there the Holy Spirit began again to work in and on me—a process that continues today. And it was there I met Gus.

Gus was a Greek man of small stature with the biggest heart I have ever seen. He was about the same age as my dad. We met at church, but our relationship really began at a Christian men's breakfast group. A discipleship program was offered in which an older man mentored and invested in the life of a younger man who wanted to grow in his relationship with the Lord. Gus became my Paul, and I was his Timothy.

Gus became like a second father, and I grew to love him very much. During that time, I began to grow in the Lord in much needed ways that still impact my life today. I am so thankful the Lord put these two men in my life. Both became important pieces of my own *When the Lost Get Found* story because they cared enough to take the time to invest in my life.

Table of Contents

Introduction. 7

Prologue: Meet Ret Law. 11

Chapter One:

Discontentment Begins in the Heart. 17

Chapter Two:

Greener Pastures. 29

Chapter Three:

The Easy Part of the Journey Is Always Downhill. 47

Chapter Four:

When All Good Things Come to a Dead End. 59

Chapter Five:

The Journey to Humiliation Station 73

Chapter Six:

When Rock Bottom Is the Best Place for You and Me. . . 81

Chapter Seven:

The Difference Between Dying and Dying to Self. 93

Chapter Eight:

That First Step Is Always the Hardest. 105

Chapter Nine:

An Unexpected Homecoming. 121

Chapter Ten:

Not Everyone Is Glad You're Home 131

Chapter Eleven:

The Final Confrontation 143

Chapter Twelve:

Saving Ret Law 155

The Invitation 161

Other Resources from Walter Spires 165

Introduction

What if you received an inheritance that made you incredibly wealthy? And what if, before realizing what had happened, you wasted *all* of it partying? And in the aftermath of being completely broke, what if you became so hungry and desperate you even contemplated the thought of dying?

As implausible as that scenario might seem, those circumstances became reality for the character that dominates much of this book.

"The Prodigal Son" is the name by which most people recognize the best-known of all Jesus' parables (stories). We find it in Luke 15. Several well-known translations (including King James, New American Standard, and English Standard) use this phrase as the heading above the verses that tell his story.

Luke 15 opens by introducing us to Jesus' audience that day. There were two groups present. The first was a collection of "tax collectors and sinners" who came to listen to Him. The second group consisted of self-righteous Pharisees and scribes (Jewish religious leaders) who watched the proceedings and criticized Jesus for hanging out with such lowlifes, "This man receives sinners and eats with them." That was beneath their dignity and another reason to hate Him.

The whole of Luke 15 contains *three* parables Jesus used to teach *both* groups that day. Each story contained something that was lost and later found: a sheep, a coin, and a son.

When the Lost Get Found focuses on the third parable. Both themes, *prodigal* and *lost*, are intertwined throughout this book as we take a deep dive into Jesus' story. Together these themes portray a young man who was *lost* in the spiritual sense but could not see it until a series of selfish, bad decisions caused him to *waste* everything he owned.

Here is an interesting test. What does the word "prodigal" mean? Most people would say they know the answer, i.e., prodigal means a runaway that later came home or something like that. Sorry, that is wrong.

The word *prodigal* derived from the mid-fifteenth century Latin words *prodigalis*, meaning "wasteful," and *prodigus*, which means "lavish" or "extravagant." So the true meaning of the adjective *prodigal* to describe this younger son in Jesus' story is *lavishly wasteful.*

The *lost prodigal son* would appear to be the main character in this book, and he is important. But I reserved that lead role for you. The truth is Jesus also had you and me in mind that day (our lives and stories) as He told what has become His most famous parable.

This book can be a quick read if you gloss over the questions, or you can chew on and digest those things that connect with you. I understand that not all of them will. I hope you choose the second path. Only then can you confront the prodigal within you, past or present, and grasp the truth that no matter how lost you are, it is never too late to be found! We call that *hope*.

My prayer is that on the other side of "the end," you find, like many of us former prodigals have, a loving Father watching and waiting for your humble return.

For Christ's sake,

Meet Ret Law

Growing up *Christian* is not without its challenges. Just ask Ret Law. He had a lot going through his high school years: popular, smart, good-looking kid. Like many from the South in his generation, Ret Law was a product of the Bible belt, brought up by God-fearing, strict parents who took the family to church every time the doors were opened. He could quote as many Bible verses as any kid in Sunday school.

Of course, at that age, most kids do not really understand them. They just memorized the words to get stars on their scorecards. Not the best motivation, but at least it had them looking things up in the Bible.

Kids raised in that kind of environment too often come to view the Bible more as a book of rules and regulations no one can keep rather than the love letter from God He intended. Let's face it: Adults also struggle with that.

The further Ret Law moved into his teens, the more he began to resent the strict world of *"thou shalt nots."* He pushed back against authority at times but tried to avoid getting in trouble. At that point in his life, he thought God was sitting around in Heaven waiting to zap people when they did something wrong—especially him.

Ret Law could not wait to *escape*, and escape he would, or so he thought. He left high school with arms full of achievement, bravado, and potential—an honor graduate, popular, great social life, and headed to a university away from home. He was eager and impatient for everything new that lay ahead, with God and church in the rearview mirror.

For most kids like Ret Law, church is another casualty in the run to independence and freedom from authority. Let's be real. Most kids do not head off to college and, upon arrival, look for a new church. They relish the idea of sleeping in on Sunday morning, especially if the "fun" of Saturday night *hangs over* until Sunday!

For the average less-than-mature freshman (who thinks he is mature), college life affords two "amenities." The first is realizing that long-sought chance to be *free*. Out from under parental authority, young men and women look for opportunities to find and express newfound freedoms. Freedom to go to whatever parties they choose and stay out all night if they feel like it. No curfews or worry of getting caught—at least not by parents.

The second amenity is *more*. They want more of just about everything college freshmen can imagine. More of the world. More new and different experiences. And too often, more than they bargained for or can handle.

The truth is most of us are more naïve at that stage of life than we would ever admit. Real maturity lags well behind *perceived* maturity. But that does not slow us down. Ret Law finally found the freedom he sought and much more.

One fairly universal area of personal growth most parents hope to see in their kids when they head off to college is that of *decision-making*: Learning to make the right choices as we prepare for life on the other side of graduation (assuming we make it that far).

Ret Law, like many freshmen, considered himself up to the challenge in every way and mature beyond his years (perception, not reality). He dove into college life headfirst, wallowing in this new environment of freedom like the proverbial pig in mud. He quickly matriculated through the basics that all incoming freshmen were introduced to by older friends from home who already knew all the ropes.

For example, Decision-Making 101 (the non-academic version) was one of the most popular courses on campus. Here critical thinking and decision-making skills had to be *crafted.*

How many beers can you drink before you throw up?

Which fraternity or sorority has the best parties?

Where do the best-looking girls (or guys) hang out?

But it was not all about social life. There were tough decisions on the academic side as well, like *which professors to avoid* and *which electives were the best GPA boosters.*

College life can be compared to a ledger. There is the credit side to which we hope to add good friends, good times, fond memories, and a good education that leads to a degree.

Then there is the debit side. Like credits, debits are earned, but they seem to cost more. They extract a greater toll on us and become very difficult to balance. Debits usually result from bad decisions that created too much of a "good thing." What seemed so good at the time resulted in failed relationships, failing grades, and worst of all (for those fortunate enough to have such a pipeline), the money from home is cut off!

Ret Law had his share of debits, but he was one of the fortunate ones. He pushed through and focused enough to receive his undergraduate degree in four years and added a graduate degree two years later. The academic side was working; the personal and spiritual sides…not so much.

The right degrees at the right time coupled with personality and contacts provided multiple options for jobs. Unfortunately, all of them would take him farther from home. Ret Law eventually ended up in a small town in which he knew only one person.

The good news was he had a great job with a new company that kept him extremely busy working long hours. But sooner or later, even young workaholics have to go home. When he did, it was to an empty apartment. There he was introduced to a new friend he never thought he would meet: *loneliness.*

All of his life, Ret Law had been surrounded by lots of friends. He was often the life of the party. Now the sounds of silence were deafening. And for the first time in his life, a sense of emptiness crept in he had never felt before.

For those whose first job out of college takes them a long way from college friends and fun, moving on can be very difficult. Maintaining relationships is hard; trying to do so over many miles compounds the challenge. It also compounds the feelings of loneliness.

Even for those who are outgoing like Ret Law, new friends are hard to come by when you move to a new town, especially a small one. Relationships take time to develop. Working day and night six-plus days a week was stimulating on the professional side but stifling on the personal one.

So Ret Law sat alone in his apartment, throwing back some beers, wondering to himself, *Is this all I have to look forward to? There must be more to life than this!*

Sometimes he would think about God. He thought about the choice he made during his college years to forego that relationship for more important things like having fun, starting a career, and "looking for love in all the wrong places," as the song lyric goes.

Maybe it was being "raised in the church" that would not allow Ret Law to get God out of his head during quiet times of loneliness. One thing was certain: He knew more *about* God and the Bible than a lot of church people. The question that haunted him now was:

Did He Really Know God?

Ret Law was like many young people whose quests for *freedom* and *more* lead them into places they never planned.

They throw off family, religion, and God. Some remain there for a season, ultimately returning to the realities of life. Some never find their way home.

We will circle back to Ret Law to learn the rest of his story on the other side of this book. Now I encourage you to read these pages written around the best-known story Jesus ever told. As you do, look for yourself in the life of the younger brother to whom I affectionately refer to throughout the book as *Prodigal.* Later, when his older brother takes center stage, you might find some things in his life with which you identify (whether you want to admit it or not).

Let's get started!

CHAPTER ONE

Discontentment Begins in the Heart

"And [Jesus] said, "A man had two sons. The younger of them said to his father, 'Father, give me the share of the estate that falls to me.' So he divided his wealth between them." Luke 15:11-12

*O*utrageous! For those raised in modern western culture, the request of the younger son, Prodigal, to receive his inheritance early may come across as a bit *presumptuous* and *bold*. Presumptuous in that he assumed the estate had enough value to warrant his asking and that he was in the will. Bold because his father was still alive. Don't inheritances usually come into consideration *postmortem*?

The truth is, to the ears of Jesus' audience that day, the younger son's request was not presumptuous or bold. *It was outrageous!*

That deserves an explanation. People knowledgeable in Old Testament family rights and traditions know the firstborn son held the loftiest position among sons and daughters considered legitimate heirs. He was called "the *firstfruits* of his father's strength" Deuteronomy 21:17, ESV. Not only did the firstborn garner the favor of his father above the other children, but he would also become the family leader after his father's death except in unusual circumstances. There was also the added financial blessing. Assuming there was an inheritance to be divided, the firstborn son received a double portion. That meant he received two shares of the estate. All other heirs received one.

The way Luke, the writer, recorded this third parable, we quickly observe that Jesus did not mince words or spend time setting up the story. He provided no background or details on Prodigal, his father, or the older brother. Rather, He went straight to the heart of the matter: *the heart of Prodigal.*

Prodigal's demand and inappropriate behavior lead us to conclude two things: Pent up *discontentment* filled his heart. He was not satisfied with what he had and where he was. He wanted more. And such a heart would lead him into *trouble.*

My first book, *Power Tools*, was based in part on my background and experience in what were referred to as personal style and behavior temperaments: how people act and react to people and things in life. Based on that experience and the brief insight Jesus provided into Prodigal, it seems clear he was *wired* much like me and other men and women who struggle with contentment. We often find ourselves looking for the next best thing, challenge, or opportunity, something we perceive as new, different, or better, a change of scenery.

Discontentment does not just surface among people like those I described. Even people typically satisfied with the *status quo* and resistant to change find themselves wrestling with contentment when they feel overlooked or taken advantage of. Regardless of personal style or temperament, when discontentment sets in, it affects all areas of our lives: *personal, professional*, and *spiritual*.

What inferences can we draw from Prodigal's heart of discontentment and this outrageous request of his father? Four negative ones came to mind:

1. Insulting. *His father was still alive.* It was the same as saying, "Father, you are dead to me. Give me my money." Such a son would not only fail to receive his inheritance, he could also be disowned—even stoned.

2. Disrespectful. "*Father, give me…*" Every Bible translation I reviewed used the same language. Prodigal made a demand, not a request. Would it have been more palatable if he asked politely? Perhaps, but keep in mind, his father was still alive. Based on the way Jesus told the story, it was clear from the beginning Prodigal had an agenda. It began with getting his share of the money *before* it was lawfully due him.

3. Shameful. Prodigal knew how this could reflect on his father and family in their community. Neighbors and friends may begin to wonder what was wrong with a father who raised such a disrespectful son. Respect and reputation were of great importance, especially in Middle Eastern cultures.

4. Indifferent. It is true we should not put too much weight on the opinions of others. But that admonition

really does not fit this example. Prodigal knew what he was demanding and the fallout that would occur for his father, family, and himself. He knew that shame from others would come his way, along with losing respect. That did not appear to be among his concerns.

Roots of Discontentment

For some of us, seeds of discontentment were sown early in our lives. Perhaps they took a long time to take root, not showing up for years. When the root of discontentment finally showed itself, we found ourselves becoming more easily frustrated with the way things were going, people in our lives, or both.

Some of us even developed what the Bible refers to as a "root of bitterness" toward those we held responsible for sowing these seeds. Examples include parents, siblings, people disguised as friends who really were not, and employers who "held us back."

The greatest biblical example of discontentment I have studied seems quite the paradox. Solomon was the wisest and richest man who ever lived. He was the king over God's people. How does such a man become overgrown with discontentment? He not only had more than anyone else, he also had everything his heart and eyes desired. Consider his words from one of the books in the Bible that he wrote:

*"All my eyes desired I did not refuse them. I
did not restrain my heart from any pleasure..."*
Ecclesiastes 2:10a

Despite having it all, the discontentment in King Solomon's
heart grew. He would have been well-served to heed his own
advice. In one proverb, he wrote:

*"Above all else, guard your heart, for everything
you do flows from it."* *Proverbs 4:23, NIV*

We know from reading about his life, King Solomon did
not "guard his heart" well. Out of his unguarded heart grew
discontentment that eventually brought down the humbled
king who began so well. It also had devastating consequences
on his family and the nation of Israel that divided into two
soon after his death. As we know, both were later conquered
by enemies.

Having considered the issues that grew from the root of
discontentment in the life of Prodigal (and Solomon), we
would be well-served to look for possible roots in our own
lives. Three come to mind: *More. Comparison. Pride.*

More

The compulsive desire for *more* plagues all of us some of
the time and some of us all of the time. It speaks loudly of
discontentment with what I have or who I am, so I want more.
More money. More stuff or toys. More out of life, a better
lifestyle, also strongly associated with more money and stuff.

That negative drive for more is not to be confused with the *healthy ambition* to improve ourselves, our position, or our circumstances. There is nothing wrong with that when accompanied by contentment as we work and wait for things to develop.

Aside from Jesus, the best example of contentment was the apostle Paul. These verses from his letter on joy provide insight into this area of his life:

> *...for I have learned to be content in whatever circumstances I am. I know how to get along with humble means, and I also know how to live in prosperity; in any and every circumstance I have learned the secret of being filled and going hungry, both of having abundance and suffering need.*
> *Philippians 4:11-12*

Comparison

Comparison is a relative of more. It has the potential to lead us into deep waters like *envy*, *jealousy*, and *bitterness*, three deadly sins. Their best chance to take root comes when our ability to obtain more becomes limited or taken away, perhaps due to financial constraints or other untoward circumstances.

Any one of the three is fully capable of producing attitudes in us so unbecoming of Christ, no one would ever guess we belong to Him. Again, the apostle Paul gave us great counsel:

> *"For we do not presume to rank or compare ourselves with some of those who commend*

themselves; but when they measure themselves by themselves and compare themselves with themselves, they have no understanding."

2 Corinthians 10:12

Pride

Pride is the antithesis of humility. Humility is one of only two adjectives Jesus used to describe Himself. (The other was gentle.) If the aim of every Christian is to become more like Jesus, as it should be, we must take to heart Paul's instruction to Timothy, a young pastor he mentored:

"But godliness actually is a means of great gain when accompanied by contentment. For we have brought nothing into the world, so we cannot take anything out of it either. If we have food and covering, with these we shall be content."

1 Timothy 6:6-8

Writing from my stage in life (and having spent decades with desperate men and women from all walks of life), I say without equivocation, pride is the most destructive of all the enemies we face in the battle for contentment. It can be as subtle as thinking we deserve more than we are given and as overt as arrogance when we boast about what we have.

The Father's Response

Despite Prodigal's outrageous and disrespectful request, the father acquiesced and divided his estate between his sons. This leaves many of us parents and former prodigals scratching our heads. Yet Jesus offered no insights into the father's thoughts and feelings.

As a parent and former prodigal, several thoughts came to mind as to why the father might have responded as he did without questioning his son. He knew his son. Perhaps he knew it was time to let Prodigal go and learn whatever life lessons God had for him. All parents have to do that at some point with their children.

For the father to refuse his son's demand may have been the right thing to do to save face in his family and culturally, but it could have built strong resentment in the young man's heart. He may have left anyway, with little or nothing to support himself.

Thus, we could make a case that the father's intentions were good because he had his son's best *long-term* interest at heart. How Prodigal's story would turn out, the father did not know. He knew, like all parents, our children have to grow up at some point, regardless of the paths they choose and how long it takes to get there, if ever. Prodigal might come home having achieved great success or never return. The father had no idea.

Was Jesus giving us a little insight into the father's heart? Or was he simply trusting God with his son's life no matter how it turned out? Jesus did not give us the answers to those questions, though we do know how the story ends.

Prodigal was about to set out on a new out venture with his inheritance in hand. The question now becomes:

How will Prodigal handle his newfound fortune?

This is a good time to pause and prayerfully consider what we have learned about Prodigal and how we can apply the lessons to our lives. Following are questions to guide you through that thought process. Please answer them honestly with an eye toward sharing your responses with others if this book is also being used to facilitate group discussion.

Questions for Discussion

1) Define *discontentment*.

_____

_____

_____

2) Four negative *inferences* were drawn from Prodigal's demand for his inheritance that revealed the conditions of his heart. Please list them below.

a. _____

b. _____

c. _____

d. _____

Did any of them trouble you more than the others? If so, briefly explain.

_____

_____

_____

_____

_____

3) Three roots of discontentment were discussed. What were they?

a. _____

b. _____

c. _____

Describe how you can identify with each and ways it may have negatively affected your life.

a. _____

_____

_____

b. _____

_____

_____

c. _____

_____

_____

CHAPTER TWO

Greener Pastures

"And not many days later, the younger son gathered everything together and went on a journey into a distant country..." Luke 15:13a

Prodigal's discontentment did not stop at getting what he demanded of his father. That was just the first step. He had a plan in mind and could not wait to get started. He wasted little time gathering his newfound wealth to set out for "a distant country." Prodigal sought *greener pastures* far from home. (Didn't we all at some point in our lives?)

Most of us are familiar with the old proverb, "Be careful what you wish for, lest it come true!" Curiosity led me to search for its origin, and to my surprise, I learned it is from Aesop's Fables. He composed some of the world's best-known collections of morality tales (circa 260 BC). That was nearly three hundred years before Jesus told this parable.

As we follow Prodigal on his journey, recounting our own along the way, we will revisit the wisdom in those words. Unfortunately, prodigals usually find that wisdom too late. It shows up as hindsight *after* important decisions have been made, and we are well on our way to those coveted greener pastures.

As Prodigal completed gathering his wealth and possessions for the journey, we can only imagine how his senses must have come alive: *the taste of excitement for what lay ahead, the smell of freedom filling his nostrils, the weight of a full money belt around his waist, and his mind filled with visions of the greener pastures ahead.* He must have been so excited.

It was not what Prodigal heard, but what he could *not* hear that must have brought a smile to his face: voices of someone telling him what to do and where to be…blah, blah, blah. Finally, he had all he needed to be successful, or so he thought.

As I considered Prodigal's imminent journey and similar exploits of my own and other prodigals, four things common to all of us, in one form or another, came to mind:

♦ Plans ♦ Freedom ♦ Money ♦ Motivation

Plans

Those of us fortunate enough to survive and recover from wasteful years can relate, at least in part, to Prodigal's state of mind as he prepared for what would become a life-changing journey. It is obvious from the way Jesus told the story that Prodigal had been thinking about this request and his plans for some time.

No doubt Prodigal would have argued he had a plan, knew where he was going (far away from home and family), and what he planned to do with his wealth. When we are young with pockets full of money, that is about all the plan we need. Right?

The Bible has a lot to say about planning. Following is a brief discussion of two types of plans and the outcomes we should expect from each.

Plans Without Prayer and Counsel

This was Prodigal's approach. *Plans without prayer and counsel* seldom slow an impatient person down, but they almost always lead to failure. Solomon, the wisest man who ever lived, had this to say:

> *"Without counsel plans fail..." Proverbs 15:22*

Isaiah, the prophet, warned Israel of planning and moving forward without God:

> *"Woe to the rebellious children, declares the Lord, who execute a plan, but not Mine..."*
> *Isaiah 30:1*

Prodigal was not the only person in the Bible who made plans without prayer and counsel. Consider these two examples of God's people planning without Him:

– Abraham and Sarah's plan to run ahead of God's plan to give them a son that created a generational enemy for His people. (Ishmael then Isaac; read in Genesis 16.)

– King David's plan for dealing with his lover Bathsheba's husband and the catastrophic effects it had on the nation of Israel and his family. (Read in 2 Samuel 11.)

I could not find good examples of prayer without counsel that ended well.

Plans with Prayer and Counsel

The Word of God provides instructions for a better way to plan. From Solomon to Jesus, we are encouraged to seek God's wisdom through prayer and the counsel of wise and godly advisors. Here are a few key Scriptures about biblical planning:

- *"Without consultation, plans are frustrated, but with many counselors they succeed."* *Proverbs 15:22*

- *"Commit your works to the LORD, and your plans will be established." Proverbs 16:3*

- *(Jesus speaking) "For which one of you, when he wants to build a tower, does not first sit down and calculate the cost to see if he has enough to complete it?" Luke 14:28*

My final counsel on *plans* is this: *God is sovereign.* He has the ultimate say in the final outcomes of our plans. That can be wonderful or painful. As Christians, we must learn to live with that even when our plans fail or do not turn out the way we hoped.

Freedom

Freedom or escape? Hard to tell what was more on the mind of Prodigal as he gathered his money and possessions. In either case, this excited young man was about to head out on his first solo "road trip." (I loved road trips during my best prodigal years. I imagine you did too.)

Where would his journey take him? All we know is he went "into a distant country," a place no one would be around to tell him what to do and (better) what he could *not* do. A place he could *do what he wanted when he wanted.* A place he would not know anyone, nor would anyone know him. In that place, he would be free from three things that "imprison" prodigals:

♦ Authority   ♦ Boundaries   ♦ Accountability

Authority

Our two-year grandson is a reminder (of years past with our three grown children) that toddlers *think* they do not need authority. "I can do it myself" was a favorite expression of my daughter. Now the shoe is on the other foot as she experiences toddlerhood with two little boys. (That brings smiles to the faces of my wife and me.)

Teenagers can be larger versions of toddlers with two additions: *larger vocabularies* (sadly) and *greater mobility.* You will not win a war of words with a teenager. And they are more adept at escaping our presence. At that stage of life, they seek freedom, defined as *independence* and *escape* from parental authority. Prodigal fit that mold. So did many of us.

God instituted authority as part of His world order during Creation. Adam and Eve learned the hard way He is serious about obedience to it. It is probably safe to say that all prodigals learned hard lessons about obedience and authority.

Unwillingness to surrender our authority to His is why many people will not come to Christ. They do not believe they need, nor do they want, a Supreme Authority in their lives. This disregard for authority leads them to reject the fact that we are all *sinners in need of a Savior.* All of us.

Prodigal's actions made it clear he wanted to escape the sphere of his father's authority. Many Bible verses speak to our need to submit to authority…with the proviso that doing so does not contradict or violate the Word of God.

The following verse from Isaiah is a great example of God's ultimate authority and how He uses it for His purposes:

> *"For this is what the LORD says, He who created the heavens, He is the God who formed the earth and made it, He established it and did not create it as a waste place, but formed it to be inhabited: 'I am the Lord, and there is no one else.'"*
> *Isaiah 45:18*

We do not always understand how God uses His authority in our lives, so He explained in Isaiah 58 that *"His ways and thoughts are higher than ours."* Ultimately as Christians, faith brings us to trust that God has our best interests in mind. The apostle Paul said it best:

> *"And we know that God causes all things to work together for good to those who love God, to*

34

those who are called according to His purpose."
Romans 8:28

Boundaries

As parents with small children, you decide to go bowling for a family fun night. Before beginning, you make one request of the person behind the counter, "Put up the gutter guards!" Only rookie parents walk their kids up to the line, give them a heavy ball, and tell them to roll it straight down the lane toward the pins. (They usually throw it, and we hope it does not crack the beautifully waxed floor!)

Failure to put up the gutter guards has predictable results. Your child bowls ball after ball into the gutters and starts to cry, "This is not fun!" You created a family night to remember, a *miserable* one!

I believe I speak for all reformed prodigals when I say it would have been nice if life came equipped with gutter guards. Alas, it did not. Even Solomon, with all of his wisdom and wealth, came to that realization. He wrote:

"Like a city that is broken into and without walls
is a man who has no control over his spirit."
Proverbs 25:28

"A city without walls" is a great description of prodigals. We often think we are smarter than the authorities. We seek, and usually find, *greener pastures* without fences, cities without walls, and plenty of open doors. No gutter guards in sight!

Experience is a great teacher. That is unfortunate when it is *bad* experience learned the hard way. God established boundaries for our lives just as He did authority. Consider His words to Jeremiah:

> *"Do you not fear Me?" declares the LORD. "Do you not tremble in My presence? For I have placed the sand as a boundary for the sea, an eternal decree, so it cannot cross over it. Though the waves toss, yet they cannot prevail; Though they roar, yet they cannot cross over it." Jeremiah 5:22*

Can you imagine if the oceans had no boundaries? We see just a small part of what that looks like during hurricanes that destroy lives and property. Noah and his family are the only people in history to experience the full impact of all such boundaries being removed. But they had an ark and the ultimate Lifeguard protecting them.

Prodigals generally hate boundaries. But when we become Christians, we begin to recognize their value. We ask the Lord to place *gutter guards* along the lanes of life we travel and teach us to respect any boundaries He places around us for our protection.

Accountability

The final freedom Prodigal sought is the most damaging of all. Most prodigals have personally experienced it. Throughout my professional and ministry lives, I witnessed it in the lives of men and women, regardless of bank balance or zip code: *no accountability.*

What is accountability? Dictionary.com defines it as: "…
the obligation to explain, justify, and take responsibility for
one's actions."

Obligation and *responsibility* are the operative words.
Obligation is a threat to the freedom of any self-respecting
prodigal. Responsibility is more of a convenience for us but
an expectation we put on others.

People without accountability in their lives are more likely
to become victims of their own thinking and reasoning.
That is a very dangerous place to find oneself. Reasoning
with yourself easily morphs into *rationalizing.* Many of us
learned the hard way that rationalizing can become what
some clever person deemed a "ration of lies."

When we are our only advisor, it is easy to talk ourselves into
actions that lead into desperate places. Our wounds are mostly
self-inflicted because we did not seek or value the counsel or
wisdom of others. Two verses helped me and helped me help
others see the value of accountable relationships:

- *"As iron sharpens iron, so one man sharpens
  another." Proverbs 27: 17*

- *"Two are better than one because they have
  a good return for their labor. For if either of
  them falls, the one will lift up his companion.
  But woe to the one who falls when there is not
  another to lift him up." Ecclesiastes 4:9-10*

Prodigal would soon learn that freedom really is not free. It always comes at a cost.

Money

Receiving his inheritance early emboldened Prodigal to pack it all up and head out for a new frontier. Money has a way of giving us confidence and a feeling of security. When we have a lot, money can make us euphoric, clouding our thinking and judgment.

Whether we have a lot of money or a little, our attitudes toward it and how we manage what we have are what matter. It has nothing to do with the size of our bank account or the zip code in which we live. The Bible has much to say about wealth and money, not just for those who are rich by the world's standards.

Here are three potential "money traps" Prodigal would have been wise to consider. However, as most of us came to realize too late, wisdom is not typically among the outstanding characteristics of prodigals.

The lure of money. A lure in fishing is used to attract, tempt, or entice a fish to take the bait. Money is the bait that attracts most people. We lose focus on other more important things in life so we can swim around the baited hook of Satan or the world, thinking we have the ability and agility to take it and run.

In the Parable of the Seeds, Jesus told us some seeds fell among thorns.

"And the one sown with seed among the thorns, this is the one who hears the word, and the anxiety of the world and the deceitfulness of wealth choke the word, and it becomes unfruitful." Matthew 13:22

It is the *deceitfulness* of wealth that lures us into places that choke this truth out of us.

The lust for money. When greedy people have a little, they want more. When they have a lot, they still want more. Solomon warned about the pursuit of wealth:

"One who loves money will not be satisfied with money..." Ecclesiastes 5:10

The apostle Paul warned his young protégé, Timothy, about this danger:

"But those who want to get rich fall into temptation and a snare and many foolish and harmful desires which plunge men into ruin and destruction" 1 Timothy 6:9

That seems like a perfect description of what happened to Prodigal and some of us.

The love of money. The Bible equates the love of money with idolatry. Not money—the *love* of money. Christians are to love God first and best. We cannot have another lover sandwiched in between Him and us.

There are many Old and New Testament verses that provide examples of this kind of idolatry. It always ended badly. The apostle Paul gave us this warning:

> *"For the love of money is a root of all sorts of evil, and some by longing for it have wandered away from the faith and pierced themselves with many griefs."* 1 Timothy 6:10

"Pierced themselves." Self-inflicted wounds, all for the sake of money. Christians are not immune to these money issues that can lead to sin and idolatry. We must be on our guard and make honoring God first the top priority in our giving, tithes, and offerings. This was not part of Prodigal's story, but it is a vital part of ours.

Motivation

Motivation answers the *why* question: *why we do what we do*. Prodigal's motivation was clear: *independence*. Prodigal wanted independence on his terms with what he perceived as a guarantee in place. He thought he had enough of his father's money to *guarantee financial freedom.* Questionable motives usually lead to disappointing or failed results.

Motives are born in our hearts. It is easier than we will admit to deceive ourselves into thinking our motives are right or unselfish. Jeremiah gave us a strong warning:

> *"The heart is more deceitful than all else and is desperately sick; Who can understand it?"*
> Jeremiah 17:9

Though "wise King Solomon" was replete with his own wrong motives and bad decisions, these words cut to the chase of the matter:

> *"All the ways of a person are clean in his own sight, but the LORD examines the motives."*
> *Proverbs 16:2*

Like all of us who have "been there and done that," Prodigal thought his motives were just fine, assuming he thought of them at all. Most of us don't in the moment.

Before we come alongside Prodigal as his journey begins, let's pause again to consider our lives, decisions we made, the results, and their consequences.

Questions for Discussion

1) Prodigal was said to have been *equipped* with four things as he began his journey. What were they?

a. _____

b. _____

c. _____

d. _____

2) Two kinds of plans were discussed. What were they? Describe each briefly.

a. _____

_____

_____

b. _____

_____

_____

List an example of *planning without God* from your life.

_____

_____

_____

List an example of *planning with God* from your life.

_____

_____

_____

3) What are the three things that *imprison* all prodigals?
   After you list each one, describe how you have struggled
   with each and any negative outcomes as a result.

a. _____

_____

_____

b. _____

_____

_____

c. _____

_____

_____

4) What are the three *money traps* that cause people to fall into sin and plans to fail?

a. _____

b. _____

c. _____

Which one do you struggle with most and why?

_____

_____

_____

5) *Motivation* answers the _____ questions. Prodigal's motive was achieving his _____ _____. It is easier than we think to _____ ourselves into thinking our motives are right or unselfish.

When you were living the prodigal dream, what were your motives, and what caused them to change?

_____

_____

_____

_____

_____

CHAPTER THREE

The Easy Part of the Journey Is Always Downhill

"...and there he squandered his estate with loose living." Luke 15:13

"...and there he squandered his property in reckless living." Luke 15:13 ESV

"...and there wasted his substance with riotous living." Luke 15:13 KJV

"...and there squandered his wealth in wild living." Luke 15:13 NIV

"...and there wasted his possessions with prodigal living." Luke 15:13 NKJV

Thus far in Jesus' story, Prodigal got his father to acquiesce to that outrageous request for his inheritance, packed his money and possessions, and hit the road for greener pastures. Thus far, Prodigal's journey had been the easy, downhill part.

From the key verse above, we learn three things: At the end of his downhill slide, Prodigal landed hard. Second, it did not take long for Prodigal to turn freedom and fortune into failure. And finally, we begin to understand how he earned the name by which he has been known for centuries: *the Prodigal Son.*

Prodigal had given no thought to how, or how quickly, he lost all the wealth his father had graciously given to him. Like a gambler at the tables at a casino, Prodigal kept rolling the dice with no thought of the consequences that lay in wait—until he had wasted all of it. There is a reason that casinos have no clocks or windows, and "adult beverages" are free as long as you play.

In Proverbs 30, King Solomon spoke of four things in life that never say, "Enough." Fire was one of them. That proverb had prodigals in mind. It was counsel most probably never heard and would likely not have paid attention to even if they had. Fire consumes everything in its path until there is nothing left, an apt description for the way Prodigal managed his wealth. Many prodigals can relate.

Jesus did not reveal the final peek into Prodigal's wasteful living until a verse near the end of this story (verse 30). There the older brother clued us in that Prodigal's loose living included reveling with prostitutes.

For me, the words Jesus chose to describe Prodigal's lifestyle brought back to mind the classic "jerk drunk" at a frat party who made a total fool of himself, finally passed out on the dance floor, and later puked his guts out in the parking lot. Perhaps that image is foreign to some, but others are chuckling, unless, of course, that person was you!

That brings us to the front end of Prodigal's downhill journey into "greener pastures." Consequences lay ahead, but before we go there, let's return again to your story.

When we compare our life stories to Prodigal's in terms of wastefulness and financial ruin, some of us identify better with his failures than others. But there are three areas *common* to all our lives in which God measures *prodigality* (wastefulness) versus *stewardship* (accountability): *treasure, time,* and *talent.*

Wasting Our Treasure

In the last chapter, we examined three "money traps" people fall prey to, each of which can lead to idolatry or worshipping our wealth. Here we consider a different point of view: *wasting it.*

The first time Jesus taught on the subject of treasure (the Sermon on the Mount), He warned of thinking about our wealth as the means for acquiring *more* in this world and of this world. He taught that we should develop an eternal perspective on any wealth, large or small, that God entrusts to us. He closed that part of His sermon with a strong statement, as poignant today as it was then:

> *"...for where your treasure is, there your heart will be also." Matthew 6:21*

The story of the rich young man in Matthew 19 was one of Jesus' best-known encounters with people concerning treasures used to teach His disciples and followers. After an exchange with the young man about how he could *earn* his way into Heaven, Jesus closed the conversation with penetrating words the man could not accept:

> *Jesus said to him, "If you wish to be complete, go and sell your possessions and give to the poor, and you will have treasure in heaven; and come, follow Me." But when the young man heard this statement, he went away grieving; for he was one who owned much property. Matthew 19:21-22*

As we read in the key verse that began this chapter, Prodigal wasted little time wasting *all* of his treasure. The question we must answer is: What are we doing with the *treasure* God has entrusted to us? Where we invest, it concerns Him the most. Are we building His kingdom or ours?

Those are tough questions that should cause us to stop and consider our answers. The easiest way to help you answer is to check your bank accounts and inspect the "payee" fields. That always reveals what we value most.

Wasting Our Time

Could it be most people don't consider time a gift because we are always running out of it? That makes it seem more like a commodity. People like Prodigal who waste their time on foolish living demonstrate they consider it of little *value*—a commodity of a sort. I want to encourage you to change your thinking.

*Time is a **gift** from God...a **currency**, not a commodity.*

Please note the two keywords in boldface in that statement. *Gifts* are things we receive for which we did not have to pay anything. Most consider them a blessing in some form for which we are thankful.

Currency has value to everyone. People who consider time a form of currency are inclined to think more carefully about where and on what we spend it. With that in mind, let's examine our time (as currency) and whether or not we are good stewards of it.

Moses wrote one of the most beautiful of all the psalms, Psalm 90. It contains many nuggets of wisdom from his experiences with God. The following verse speaks to treasuring time and spending it wisely:

> *"So teach us to number our days, that we may present to You a heart of wisdom." Psalm 90:12*

It is interesting to note how Moses learned the value of time. He spent his first forty years as a prince of Egypt, living a life of wealth and pampering. Then his life changed radically. He spent the next forty years hiding in the desert from those same Egyptians who wanted to kill him. Finally, he spent his last forty years wandering in the desert with millions of whining Jews. God taught him many lessons during those seasons of life, one of which was learning to value the time he had and not taking it for granted.

That verse speaks to a sense of urgency we need to develop regarding our time on earth and learning what God has for us while we are here. Each day matters to God. He gives us a limited number, so we must learn to use them wisely.

The apostle Paul taught many lessons to the Christians in Ephesus. One of those spoke directly to the issue of use of time/time management:

> *"So then, be careful how you walk, not as un-wise people but as wise, making the most of your time, because the days are evil."*
> Ephesians 5:15-16

Paul knew then (circa 60 AD) what we know today: The times and days in which we live are continually increasing in evil. Jesus said it has been that way since the days of Noah, after the flood that rid the world of evil...for a while (Matthew 24:37).

What does that mean for us? With whatever remaining time God gives us, and while we have the freedom to do so, we need to be good stewards. For Christians, that means investing time in our relationship with Christ, making quality time for our marriages and families, and managing the time we allocate to other things from work to hobbies.

My final thought on this topic is this: *the return of Christ is imminent*. On several occasions, Jesus spoke about the temporary nature of time and this world. Here is one example:

> *"We must carry out the works of Him who sent Me as long as it is day; night is coming, when no one can work." John 9:4*

The works to which Jesus referred are *sharing the love of God in Christ* (evangelism) and *making disciples.* Christian, how much of your time is invested in Kingdom work?

Wasting Our Talent

So many people waste this one more than the others. I love to see faces of people who think they have no talent light up when I explain that God gave them gifts that manifest themselves as talents.

We reside in the greater Nashville area, known mostly for the incredible level of musical talent. Some were fortunate to get the break that changed their lives forever, at least in terms of fame and fortune. Others labor in jobs like serving tables in restaurants or parking cars while they wait for the opportunity to showcase their talents.

Throughout my years of ministry, I've also met very talented people in prison, rescue missions, and among the homeless. Even I have talents! God does not exclude anyone.

Perhaps the best biblical account of this amazing *gifting from God* is recorded in the following passage from Exodus when He told Moses who He wanted to build His tabernacle:

> *Now the LORD spoke to Moses, saying, "...I have filled him [one of the workers] with the Spirit of God in wisdom, in understanding, in knowledge, and in all kinds of craftsmanship, to make artistic designs for work in gold, in sil-ver, and in bronze, and in the cutting of stones*

for settings, and in the carving of wood, that he
may work in all kinds of craftsmanship...in the
hearts of all who are skillful I have put skill..."

Exodus 31:1-6

God was delighted to place these talents in the hearts of those He called *skillful*. The use of their talents was meant to bring pleasure to themselves and glory to God.

In any community, we don't need to look hard to find artisans of all kinds. *Artists with brush or pen. Leather crafters. Wood and metal workers. Chefs and those with culinary skills. Gardeners of all kinds. People skilled in other areas using their hands, brilliant minds, or special hearts.* I repeat, no one has been left out!

Following is a great example of one to whom God gave a specific talent that was used just as He intended: *for His glory*. The man was Eric Liddell, a Scottish missionary to China.

As a young man, Eric was an Olympic runner who won a gold medal in the 1924 Paris Olympics. If you have never watched the 1981 movie, *Chariots of Fire*, you need to. Eric was a deeply committed Christian whose plan was to head to China after the Olympics. He refused to run on Sunday, which took him out of his best race. He went on to win in another event.

One of Eric's more notable quotes has two parts we need to note.

- "I believe that God made me for a purpose." He said that in reference to being a missionary to

54

China. He went on to say what most remember.

- "He also made me fast. And when I run, I feel His pleasure."

Whatever your talents may be, use them! You will find they bring pleasure and peace to your life. For some, their use becomes a sanctuary. For others, it provides an escape from a world that can be brutal and unkind.

Do not let anyone hold you back or put you down for doing so. Some of the happiest people in the world are those who do not make much money but found ways to use their talents and enjoy life in their lane, not the fast lane. *All for the glory of God*!

Questions for Discussion

1) Why does the easiest part of any journey that leads us into trouble always seem downhill?

_____

_____

_____

2) Prodigal lost no time wasting all he had. Are there parts of your story that relate to that part of his?

_____

_____

_____

3) What are the three areas of wastefulness vs. stewardship that were discussed? Take some time to consider whether you are *wasting* or *stewarding* each area in your life. Briefly record your thoughts on areas that need work and how you can improve.

a. _____

_____

_____

b. _____

_____

_____

c. _____

_____

_____

CHAPTER FOUR

When All Good Things Come to a Dead End

"Now when he had spent everything, a severe famine occurred in that country, and he began to be impoverished." Luke 15:14

From greedy to needy. These words would make a fitting subtitle for Prodigal's journey to this point. Jesus did not fill in the blanks to give us specifics of what He meant by *riotous living.* But we do know that at the end of all his fun, Prodigal had nothing in his pockets but air and lint. Some of us have been there.

Prodigal was broke with nowhere to turn, alone in a foreign land. For the first time in his life, he found himself in another new place—a dead end.

Bad Decisions Followed by Bad Timing

There is never a good time to find yourself broke and without options, especially in a strange country where you have no family or friends. To complicate matters, the timing of Prodigal's demise was particularly bad. Not only had the security of his material world completely collapsed, but it also happened just before the land was struck by a famine.

Most people know famines are times when a region experiences long periods of drought that dry up the food supply: Crops wither and die. People can starve to death. Jesus called this one a *severe famine*. He described it as such so those hearing His story would understand the desperation of the Prodigal's situation.

The convergence of those two calamities—*completely broke* and *living in a severe famine*—put Prodigal in the middle of a "perfect storm." His situation was akin to a man rowing across a large lake, unaware a huge storm approached. Once surrounded by the storm, he realized he was too far out to turn back, helpless with no control over the consequences.

Consequences always follow decisions: good and bad. It is noteworthy that the first of Prodigal's calamities resulted from things he controlled. It was *self-inflicted*. He chose to squander his wealth, albeit unintentionally. The second calamity was beyond his control: a natural disaster.

Jesus told us the worst of Prodigal's consequence was staring him in the face: "...*he began to be impoverished*." Another Bible translation reads, "*he began to starve*." Poverty and starvation were not among Prodigal's thoughts and plans before he left the comforts of home.

It is important for us to see a clear picture of how far Prodigal had fallen, the consequences of his bad decisions. Before leaving home, he was the son of a wealthy landowner who loved and provided for him. Now he was a desperate young man, broke and alone in a foreign land; even his food supply was about to run out.

Time to hit the pause button again on Prodigal's story and return to yours. Let's turn our attention to two types of circumstances Prodigal faced that also confront us:

- *Things he controlled*

- *Things beyond his control*

Areas We Control

1) Attitudes

In our world of information overload and constant bombardment from social and other media outlets, many people feel they have little control over things in their lives. Some feel they have lost complete control. I have good news for you.

Attitude is one area in your life over which you have complete control. We choose how we feel about things that happen to us and around us and how we respond. We choose how we interact with and treat other people, regardless of how they treat us.

"Attitudes determine outcomes" is a popular saying among motivational speakers and others who generally see the "glass as half full." I always thought it is more accurate to say, "Attitudes *can* determine outcomes." Other things can get in the way.

The way Jesus introduced Prodigal made it easy for us to conclude he had an attitude problem—a bad one. His demand of his father demonstrated he considered himself above or before others and wanted things his way. That led to outcomes he never envisioned but perhaps deserved. The same could be said for some of us when we reflect on his story and the ways in which it parallels our own.

Just as Prodigal's behavior indicated, when we become *self-absorbed,* we are much more prone to become *self-indulgent.* That becomes a very undesirable combination when it exerts strong influence or control over how we live and interact with others. In addition, such self-centeredness affects how we make decisions.

2) Decisions

Decisions we control flow from attitudes in our minds, feelings in our hearts, and information before our eyes. We make dozens of decisions every day. Some are almost unconscious, while others require thoughtful consideration.

We make personal decisions about life, money, and relationships, interpersonal and spiritual. We make professional decisions concerning vocations and careers, what we want to do and where we want to do it.

You may be familiar with the phrase, "making a decision in a vacuum." The decision-maker does not seek or receive outside input before moving forward, confident he or she has the intelligence or enough information to go it alone. Prodigal fell into this category.

We read in chapter two how his disastrous outcomes resulted from the bad decision-making process he used: *listening only to the voice inside his head.* That goes against all sound biblical wisdom. King Solomon offered this counsel:

> *"Where there is no guidance the people fall, but in an abundance of counselors there is victory."*
> Proverbs 11:14

Like Prodigal, we have all made bad decisions and suffered the consequences. That is part of life. We have also made good ones. Let's be practical about this. There are times it makes sense to take the time to seek outside counsel, and other times, that is not possible.

Following is what I refer to as a *decision-making screen* that contains three questions. I have found it helpful throughout many years of making decisions of all kinds, personal and professional:

- *What is my motive (or agenda) in this decision?*

- *Does the Bible speak to this matter, directly or indirectly?*

- *How will this decision affect my relationships? God, wife and family, others.*

From Adam and Eve to the present, the failure of people to own their decisions, good and bad, created many of our world's problems. Some led to wars; others to conflicts and disasters of many kinds. The same may be said for problems within the church. Contributing factors range from interpersonal conflicts among leadership to loss of focus on the mission by taking our eyes off Jesus.

Two final words on decisions we control. *Own them*! Regardless of the outcome, we must acknowledge responsibility for our decisions and the consequences that accompany them.

Areas We Do Not Control

For some people, this is a sad truth: There are people and things in life over which we have no control. We have to learn to live with that. Easier said than done! Now my confession: I'm a reforming "control freak," and that made this section more difficult to write! But I recognize the value in doing so for others who struggle in that area.

Being in control is important to many people. How important depends on factors like personality type and the environment in which you were raised. Studying Prodigal's story and those of other men and women in the Bible, I came to the conclusion there are three areas over which we have no control:

Others ■ *Nature* ■ *God*

Attitudes and Actions of Others

Consider the apostle Paul. He was a faithful messenger of the Lord after his conversion. His passion became taking the gospel to the Gentiles around his world with great expectations that men and women would hear it as the truth and receive Christ as Savior. Some did, many more did not.

The Jews were particularly opposed to Paul's teaching because they had also opposed Jesus and were instrumental in having Him put to death. Their attitudes and actions demonstrated they had the same intentions for Paul:

"But Jews came from Antioch and Iconium, and having won over the crowds, they stoned Paul and dragged him out of the city, supposing him to be dead." Acts 14:19

Paul knew many would reject him and his message that Jesus is the Messiah. He had no control over that, so he had to accept it. Yet, we know Paul was undeterred in his mission. He remained faithful to that which God called him, despite the suffering he incurred.

Our challenge is to respond as Paul did: understand that we cannot control what others think and say about us or how they behave toward us. Our task is to move on with an attitude of gratitude (to God), doing our best to leave anger and resentment behind. Easier said than done! In fact, it is only possible by living under the power of the Holy Spirit.

Nature

After Prodigal arrived in that distant country, he encountered one thing that he did not expect over which he had no control: a severe famine. From what we read, to his credit, Prodigal simply dealt with it. Even the worst control freaks among us know we have no control over natural disasters. Don't we?

But even when we have no physical control over things like famines or other natural disasters, we are not helpless. Here is one great example.

We have resided in middle Tennessee for nineteen years. In May 2010, we experienced what became known as the greatest flood in the area's recorded history. It rained for many days, causing every river, tributary, and creek to rise high swiftly over their banks, rapidly flooding many areas, causing loss of life and billions in property damage.

Many homes were underwater. Buildings floated off their foundations. Thousands lost all they owned. It is a great understatement to only say it was devasting. There was one thing all of us had in common: *No control.*

Many of us learned a valuable lesson. Though we cannot control nature and how it adversely affects our lives, we *can* control our attitudes toward whatever happens, even when the outcome is so devastating.

Responses from those affected spanned a broad range as they always do when natural disasters strike. Fear. Anxiety. Anger. Depression. Discouragement. Relief. Those who best handled the disaster did so by having an *attitude of gratitude*. They were thankful their lives were spared. Despite all the devastation, it could have been worse.

Christians, like many others, offered comfort to those affected by physically helping clear and clean things and financially through donations. But we had one more thing to offer that the others could not: Prayers to our God Who cares about every need we have and words of comfort like these from King David's psalms:

> *"I sought the Lord and He answered me and delivered me from all my fears."* Psalm 34:4

We cannot control nature. We can control our attitudes when the consequences of natural disasters adversely affect us. And we can go for help to the One Who created it…

God

Sad to admit that true control freaks even want to control God! Seems ridiculous, doesn't it? But control freaks are not the only people who want to control God in certain circumstances. *All* of us do.

Consider these questions: *Have you ever told God what He should do? Have you ever told Him when He should do it, even scolded Him when He was late*? That suggests we think we know more than He does, and our timing is better. While most scoff at such a suggestion, honest people admit it is true. There are times in our lives we even try to control God!

The first and best example of one who seemed justified to attempt to do so is Job. If you are not familiar with his story, here are the short notes. Job was a righteous man before God. Satan challenged God to let him have his way with Job. So God allowed Satan to destroy Job's property, family, and health, but he could not take Job's life.

Things got so bad, Job's wife suggested that he "curse God and die." Three friends came along to *comfort* Job but ended up trying to figure out what he did that was so bad God would cause all of this to happen to him. Who needs friends like that?

Job defended himself on every front. We read early in his story these words that must take root in the heart of every Christian if we are to live in a right relationship with our God:

"...in all this Job did not sin with his lips." Job 2:10

At the end of the story, Job again declared his faith and trust in God, despite all he lost. We know God restored two-fold all that had been taken away (Job 42:10). That kind of ending does not always happen for us. In fact, it usually does not.

Our lesson? Let God be God and walk in faith believing He has our absolute best in mind in all that comes our way— no matter what the world thinks or says about it or us. The apostle Paul taught us this precious truth:

"And we know that God cause all things to work together for good to those who love God, to those who are called according to His purpose"
Romans 8:28

The easy part is reading that verse. The hard part is giving up our control and submitting to the sovereign authority of God our Father, Who always knows best!

Questions for Discussion

1) Prodigal was caught in what was referred to as "a perfect storm," the convergence of two factors. What were they?

a. _____

b. _____

Give an example of how bad decisions you made were compounded by external factors and put you in a bad place.

_____

_____

_____

2) _____ always follow decisions, good or bad.

a. Since the only consequences of Prodigal's decisions were bad, can you share any bad consequences of past decisions you would change if you could?

_____

_____

_____

b. One absolute necessity after we make a decision (regardless of the outcome) is this.

We must _____ our decision and its consequences.

3) What are the two areas in our lives we *can* control?

a. _____

b. _____

If you disagree or can add others, please explain why and add them below.

_____

_____

_____

4) What are the three areas in our lives we cannot control? Add any comments from personal experiences, good and bad.

a. _____

_____

_____

b. _____

_____

_____

c. _____

_____

_____

CHAPTER FIVE

The Journey to Humiliation Station

"So he went and hired himself out to one of the citizens of that country, and he sent him into his fields to feed pigs. And he longed to have his fill of the carob pods that the pigs were eating, and no one was giving him anything." Luke 15:15-16

Some people seemed destined to succeed. Alana was one of *those* people. She was incredibly smart, best in her class in terms of grades. She was very proud of her intelligence, sometimes to the point she came across a little on the arrogant side.

There was no challenge too great for her; nothing could stand in her way or slow her down. Alana, of course, graduated from college *magna cum laude*. As far as people could see, she had no flaws, and there was certainly nothing to keep her from medical school and pursuing her dream of becoming a surgeon.

With Alana, the problem was not what people could see; it was what they could *not* see below the surface. When I thought about Alana's story, the *Titanic* immediately came to mind. Everything on the surface looked great. *Titanic* was the most magnificent ship ever built in that era, considered *unsinkable*...until she did.

Alana was like that. Everything *appeared* to be going great on the surface. But medical school can be one of the most taxing endeavors a young woman or man can undertake with long hours studying, too little sleep, fierce competition, and temptation.

The competitive spirit in Alana drove her to be the smartest and best. After all, to this point in her life, she took great pride in being at the top of her class. Now she was at a different level. The other students were as smart, some smarter, and the stakes were higher. She had to remain at the top of her class if she was going to get the right internship and opportunity to become a surgeon.

I am all too familiar with people who arrive at stations in their lives when the pressure becomes so great that they no longer just bend; they break. At that point, the challenge to find a quick advantage or easier way out begins to steal their ability to judge things rationally.

Too often, drugs provide that escape. But they are not an escape. They are a road into deeper, darker places. Alana found herself in such a place.

As we saw with Prodigal, bad decisions are often followed by bad consequences and lead people into desperate places. Some find their way out; others do not. Alana was not one of the fortunate ones.

As her addiction worsened, she was unceremoniously dismissed from medical school. This was completely unforeseen—her worst nightmare. She had no backup plan, nor did she have a place to go. But there are always places to go, just not where you planned or would ever choose to find yourself.

When the money ran out, as it always does, she was out…out on the street among people not nearly as smart as she was, but with one thing in common: *bad decisions*. The last time Alana was seen, she was on a street corner holding a sign that read, "Even smart people do stupid things. Please help!"

She was embarrassed and humiliated, hoping someone would care enough to help.

***

"Desperate times call for desperate measures." That quote has its origins in a similar phrase spoken by Hippocrates concerning the treatment of extreme diseases. Prodigal qualified as desperate, broke with no prospects in a foreign country.

Let's give Prodigal *some* credit. After a season of utterly wasting his life and fortune, he looked for a job instead of becoming a beggar. He may have been better off begging!

In the two verses used to introduce this chapter, Jesus provided a few details about what Prodigal did and how he felt. From them, we observe four signs that bear evidence of the negative changes affecting his life, all consequences of his bad decisions made along his way.

1) Desperation

"So he went and hired himself out to a citizen of that country."

Prodigal went to work for a *Gentile*. That may not seem like a big deal to those of us who are also Gentiles. That simply meant anyone who is not a Jew in biblical terminology. But to Jews, Gentiles were considered sinners and unholy people and not to be associated with. The fact that Prodigal was completely broke with no prospects was embarrassing. But going to work for a Gentile was a neon sign that flashed: "Desperation."

Prodigal's circumstances, *broke without prospects of work*, created a sense of urgency to find work and change his circumstances. Severe hunger has a way of doing that to people.

2) Humiliation

"...and he sent him into his fields to feed pigs."

First, desperation forced Prodigal to take work from a Gentile. Now to add insult to injury, Prodigal was sent to do a job more loathsome than any he could have imagined—*feeding pigs!*

You do not have to be an expert in Jewish law to know that swine were among the unclean animals, so much so that Jews today still do not eat pork. Here is God's command to Moses:

> *"And the pig, for though it has a divided hoof,*
> *and so it shows a split hoof, it does not chew cud;*

it is unclean to you. You shall not eat any of their flesh nor touch their carcasses; they are unclean to you." Leviticus 11:7-8

Feeding and looking after pigs. For a young Jewish man, life could not sink any lower except for one more thing Jesus told us about Prodigal's state of mind.

3) Envying pigs

"And he longed to have his fill of the carob pods that the pigs were eating..."

Envying pigs...now *that* is hunger! Jesus used these verses to capture the complete attention of the Jews listening that day. They would have been horrified at the thought of being put in a position where they had to work for a Gentile *and* feed his pigs! Jesus took them even lower. He said this humiliated Jewish son was so destitute that he *lusted* after the food thrown before pigs.

Most of us cannot relate to this depth of hunger and despair. Throughout my years of ministry, I have encountered many men and women who have been there; some still are. Whose fault it was really does not matter when someone finds themselves stranded at such a place in life. They do not dwell on how they got there. Rather, they quickly turn their attention to where the next meal is coming from.

That was certainly true for Prodigal. The question now became: Could he find anyone to help? That was quickly answered.

4) No one cared

"...and no one was giving him anything."

This was the final insult. No one gave a %&$% about Prodigal or his circumstances. Why should they? He was a Jew in a Gentile country. Maybe they knew his story, maybe not. If they did, they probably thought he was a foolish young man who deserved what he got! His wounds were self-inflicted.

The bottom line for Prodigal was this: No one cared he was starving, a fact that had become painfully obvious. We sense a twinge of *hopelessness* in his words.

Loss of hope is something I have seen in the eyes of women and men or heard in their voices. Such is the plight of many on our streets today. *Hopeless* was probably the last feeling of people whose final decision in life should have been reserved for God alone: men and women who took their own lives.

As one who teaches hope and breathes it into the lives of men and women from all walks of life, regardless of zip code, this grieves my spirit. We know that real hope is *eternal hope* found only in a relationship with Jesus Christ. But hearing those words is not enough.

Men and women who have been utterly humiliated by the consequences of bad decisions in their lives look first for physical comfort before spiritual: food and escape from the cold and damp to a dry or warm place to sleep or find shelter. They are not thinking about eternity; they are thinking about surviving *now*.

If Prodigal's life was a train ride, we would all agree he had indeed arrived at *Humiliation Station*!

Questions for Discussion

1) In the space below, list the four signs in Prodigal's life discussed in this chapter that reveal the hard-earned place he landed after his season of squandering. Describe how (or if) you can relate to each. What were the things that took you there or a similar place?

a. _____

_____

_____

b. _____

_____

_____

c. _____

_____

_____

d. _____

_____

_____

2) Prodigal found this new "community" he was now in very uncaring. Christians are called to be the "hands and feet" of Jesus in our world, beginning in our communities. James encouraged and admonished us to demonstrate

that in deeds, not words (James 2:15-16). A number of comments were made about the plight of the poor and homeless in our communities. What is your attitude toward needy people of all races and creeds in your community? Would they testify that you care about their plight? Do your actions demonstrate that you do? Give an example or two.

_____

_____

_____

CHAPTER SIX

When Rock Bottom Is the Best Place for You and Me

"But when he came to his senses…" Luke 15:17

These seven words of Jesus became of greater interest to me when I began *studying* this parable rather than just *reading* it. That phrase is the *inflection point* of the entire story where the narrative changes direction. They imply Prodigal finally owned the reality he had created completely on his own; no one else to blame.

It is interesting to note that Jesus did not hint or suggest in any way Prodigal had some sort of spiritual epiphany or angelic visitation to arrive at this *inflection point* in his life. He simply said Prodigal "came to his senses" *on his own.* The question is:

What caused Prodigal to "come to his senses"?

To answer this question and frame the rest of the story, we need to consider where Prodigal had been and where he sat now. Three reasons he *came to his senses* stood out to me:

- *The consequences of his bad decisions*

- *Learning the hard way that freedom can become a prison*

- *The view from "rock bottom"*

Consequences of Bad Decisions

Desperate. Destitute. Hungry. Homeless. Helpless. In previous chapters, we followed the exploits of Prodigal as he made bad decisions. These five words describe the final resting place for Prodigal as the outbound part of his journey came to a sad end.

Bad decisions have a way of compounding, creating *the snowball effect*. Prodigal's bad decisions rolled up on one another until the "snowball" finally crashed into something bigger or harder and broke into pieces. He experienced a great fall of Humpty Dumpty proportions!

Learning the Hard Way"Freedom Can Become a Prison"

This is common among men and women in prison. Many are there because of bad decisions that involve overstepping the boundaries of their freedom. Some never knew boundaries growing up. Others had boundaries but chose to ignore them, thinking they were entitled to something without working for it or would never have to face any consequences.

They failed to learn that freedom comes with *responsibility.* The converse is just as true. *Irresponsibility* often leads to loss of freedom. For those in prison, bad decisions cost them their freedom. Prodigal was one of the fortunate ones. He remained *free* despite his bad decisions. But he landed in such a hard place that we could reasonably assert he really was not free at all.

The View from "Rock Bottom"

Prodigal left home brimming with self-confidence, high hopes, and a share of the family wealth to fund his exploits. The future was bright, or so it seemed. But Prodigal's dreams never materialized. High hopes were replaced with the lowest lows. His new reality was a place familiar to some of us: that metaphorical place we call "rock bottom."

It is very reasonable to believe Jesus brought Prodigal to this hard place to illustrate the impact and consequences bad company and worse decisions have on our lives. This part of His story was pointed in the direction of all the "sinners" in the audience.

Like Prodigal, many of us have gotten so caught up in ourselves it became nearly impossible to *come to our senses* until we finally hit our own *rock bottom*.

The phrase *rock bottom* is said to have its roots in agriculture. When a farmer was digging in his fields and hit bedrock, he could not go any lower. Bedrock was considered impenetrable. Thus, the phrase *hitting rock bottom* was born. Over the years, its use broadened into other applications like the one that describes Prodigal's place in life. He *could not sink any lower,* n*or could things get any worse.*

All of us have faced (or will face) times in our lives when bad decisions and overextended freedom led us to our own views of rock bottom. When I considered *rock bottom* experiences from my own life and those of people I have known or served in ministry, three types came to mind: *personal, professional, and spiritual.*

Personal Rock Bottom

Extreme examples. During many years of ministry, I have seen "up close and personal" too many examples of men and women at *rock bottom*. Terrible decisions resulted in rock bottoms like substance abuse, addiction, and even time in prison. Many desperately seek a way out. Sadly, others are content to remain there.

Closer to home, money problems often initiate a downhill slide. Once in motion, the slide is facilitated by bad decisions that, left unchecked, spiral us downward into financial despair. The ultimate landing place from such dire financial circumstances is homeless on the street, the same place Prodigal sat.

Perhaps the greatest contributors to that most undesirable personal landing place are *failed relationships*. Marriages fail and end in divorce. Parenting failures can drive children into shells or rebellion, both of which may lead to marital and family failures. Children make terrible life choices that create tremendous stress in a family, some of which destroy their own futures.

Then there are the consequences. Consequences of failed relationships are well-known. They lead men, women, and children to places we consider rock bottom: *clinical depression, substance abuse, divorce, crime, financial ruin, isolation…and even the hardest of all, suicide.*

Professional Rock Bottom

Many men and women today are married to their work and careers. Some take a more balanced approach to life, and others consider work a means of supporting their hobbies. Over the last half-century, too much self-esteem has become tied to one's work. That makes losing a job one of the greatest causes of stress in our country.

Losing one's job for any reason can make it hard to cope with life. Plant closings or relocations. Layoffs due to the economy. Firings, with or without cause. All result in loss of income and remove our ability to provide for personal and family needs. The fallout often brings great emotional stress, the effects of which are far-reaching.

The Western world has moved beyond being consumer-driven to consumptive excess that produces a sort of *co-dependency* on buying new "toys" of all kinds. When employment goes away, so does buying power. People addicted to spending and consumption act like nothing has changed and use credit (while it lasts) to spend themselves into deep pits of debt.

Others become dependent on their families or the government. Some of the latter begin to feel a sense of *entitlement* and stop looking for employment.

Finally, there are people like Prodigal, who take any job they can to survive even if it feels beneath their experience and skillsets. As we saw with Prodigal, this can be humiliating. Men and women who find themselves at a place in life where they cannot find employment or their skill sets are no longer of value to an organization agree on one thing: They hate the view from *rock bottom.*

Spiritual Rock Bottom

As bad as things get when we find ourselves at relational, financial, or job-related rock bottom, one place is lower and harder: *spiritual rock bottom.* All of us have been at spiritual rock bottom at some point in our lives. (I include those who reject all forms of *spirituality* because they have known this even though they may deny its existence or call it something else.)

What does *spiritual rock bottom* look like? The better question is: What does spiritual rock bottom *feel* like? It feels like a downward spiral into the depths of despair that progresses as follows:

- *God does not answer my prayers.*

- *God does not hear my prayers.*

- *God does not care.*

- *Who needs God?*

- *There is no God.*

Emma understood that spiritual death spiral. Her family attended church, but it never meant much to her. Boring sermons and singing songs, mostly written by people who had been dead for centuries, failed to inspire her. She believed in God because she never gave Him enough consideration not to. After all, almost everyone believes in God, regardless of whether or not they know anything about Him.

Emma was a senior in college when she received a call from her dad. Bad news. Her mother had been diagnosed with cancer, and the prognosis was not good. Emma was devastated. She felt helpless and desperate. Being close to her mother made the thought of losing her to cancer unbearable.

Bad news of this kind often causes people to go to their knees and pray. Emma began to cry out to this God she knew only by name to heal her mother. She even asked others to pray for her mother's healing. If He could heal, why not ask? Nothing to lose, right?

More bad news. The cancer continued to spread. Emma began to think that God did not hear her prayers. As her mother began to physically deteriorate, Emma decided God did not care about her mother's disease. Maybe He did not care about either of them.

Sadly, as is the case for many cancer victims, the disease was detected too late to slow and send it into remission. Emma's mother was put under hospice care. That sent Emma deeper into her spiritual spiral. *Who needs God?* she thought. What kind of God would let this horrible disease take her mother's life in such a horrible way?

Emma's mother was not the only one who died that day she finally succumbed to cancer. God also died in the heart and mind of Emma. The downward spiral was complete; she had arrived at her spiritual rock bottom.

In life, there are times we just do not and cannot understand God's reasoning. One of the hardest things for people to grasp when things are going downhill is this: *God is God, and we are not.* He even spoke to that through the prophet Isaiah when the people of Israel wondered what God was doing, or not:

> *"'For My thoughts are not your thoughts, nor are your ways My ways,'" declares the LORD. 'For as the heavens are higher than the earth, so are My ways higher than your ways and My thoughts than your thoughts.'"*
> Isaiah 55:8-9

In His sovereignty, there are times God takes us to or allows us to hit rock bottom. For some, rock bottom is often the place at which we lean in and listen to God or continue to walk our own way. Unfortunately, others who hit rock bottom are paralyzed by tragedy or so burdened by its weight that they are unable to move at all.

That was the case for Emma. Her spiritual wounds were too fresh, too burdensome to allow her to move at all, much less toward God. As Christians, such times *should* move us closer to our Savior because in Him, we have placed our hope no matter what happens. And we pray for the Emmas God puts in our lives to find that hope during times of tragic loss and turn back to His comforting love.

The Best Place to Be

For people like Prodigal, hitting rock bottom causes them to come to their senses. There is just something about failure that makes us better suited to handle success. Something about utter humiliation that creates a humble heart. Something about the feeling that God has abandoned us that makes us desperate enough to pursue Him.

God is intentional in everything He does or allows. He is intentional about you and me. Otherwise, why were we the only beings in creation made in His image? When we forsook His love and deserted Him, why did He remain steadfast in His love for us? And why in the world would He not only allow but intentionally send His only Son, Jesus, to be a human sacrifice to redeem repentant souls from our sins that bore the death penalty? Why indeed?

My dear friends, we may not like the journey that takes us there or all we learn about ourselves once we land, but this I know: There are appointed times in our lives during which God wants to get and hold our attention. It is during those times I can say unequivocally: *That is when rock bottom is the best place to be.*

Questions for Discussion

1) Personal rock bottom

List an example of one you have seen or experienced.

_____

_____

_____

How did you "come to your senses"?

_____

_____

_____

2) Professional rock bottom

List an example of one you have seen or experienced.

_____

_____

_____

How did you "come to your senses"?

_____

_____

_____

3) Spiritual rock bottom

List an example of one you have seen or experienced.

_____

_____

_____

How did you "come to your senses"?

_____

_____

_____

CHAPTER SEVEN

The Difference Between Dying and Dying to Self

But when he came to his senses, he said, "How many of my father's hired laborers have more than enough bread, but I am dying here from hunger! I will set out and go to my father, and will say to him, 'Father, I have sinned against heaven, and in your sight; I am no longer worthy to be called your son; treat me as one of your hired laborers.'" Luke 15:17-19

In the last chapter, we concluded that hitting *rock bottom* was the best thing that could have happened to Prodigal. For the first time in Jesus' story, we find him in a good place: *He came to his senses.* As his story continued, we read that he began to have the *right* conversations with himself. What do I mean by *right* conversations? *Honest ones*!

Learning to have honest conversations with ourselves may sound a bit strange to some. Talking to yourself? But as we will learn about Prodigal in these verses, that process can have incredible healing effects provided they come from a heart of contrition like the one he had developed.

That is the *being honest with ourselves* part. Otherwise, we may fall back into or continue giving ourselves bad advice as Prodigal did at the beginning of his story. Solomon had this to say about fools listening to their own advice:

> *"There is a way which seems right to a person,*
> *but its end is the way of death."* Proverbs 14:12

That is a very appropriate thought for how someone facilitates the way to rock bottom.

With the three verses that begin this chapter, Jesus began to show us the transformation taking place within Prodigal. He was finally beginning to face his new realities that were becoming increasingly clearer as he looked up from the bottom. It was as if they were asking him, "Now that you finally 'get it,' where do we go from here?"

To answer that question, let's examine these new realities and how Prodigal responded to them. When we examine what he said and the full context of his journey to this point, three stood out to me that I thought would be worth deeper consideration.

Reality #1: Prodigal knew his wounds were no one's fault but his own.

This is a very powerful realization and admission. How did I arrive at that conclusion? It is what Prodigal did *not* say. He refrained from doing what most people would do (including you and me): start playing the blame game!

Old Prodigal might have blamed his troubles and misfortunes on people he met in that *far country* where he traveled and squandered everything. Instead, we surmise that *Rock Bottom*

Prodigal accepted responsibility for his poor choices and the miserable position and place he found himself as a result.

For many years, I have been involved in ministry to numerous groups of men and women: *prisoners, addicts, homeless, those in recovery programs*, and *church people*. Among them, I identified two groups that struggle a lot when it comes to how they respond when trouble and adversity come calling. I refer to them as *blamers* and *shamers*.

Blamers first look to assign fault or responsibility to something or someone else when things go badly. When they get into trouble or find themselves at rock bottom, they can be heard to say, "I was a victim of circumstances, in the wrong place at the wrong time." Or, "If he or she had not done that to me, this would have never happened." With blamers, it is never their fault.

Shamers sit at the other end of the spectrum. They have little to no self-esteem and too readily accept fault or blame even when it is not theirs to own. Their innate sense of failure prevents them from moving forward in life because they fail to recognize that being so accepting of people without question is a form of *enabling*. That leads to worse problems.

As we read in the conversation with himself, Prodigal was looking ahead, not back. He did not blame his situation or circumstances on others. Neither did he engage in a "pity party" or beat himself up over what he had done and where he was at this point in his life. His words intimate to us he owned his self-inflicted issues and was preparing to move on.

Reality #2: The gravity of his situation:
not just at a dead-end but dying.

In verse seventeen, we read Prodigal's own assessment of his dire predicament:

"How many of my father's hired laborers have more than enough bread, but I am dying here from hunger!"

Reality does not get more *real* than impending death. Fear of death is one of the great motivators in life to cause people to want to change their circumstances if they can. In my ministry, at times, I have come across men and women whose bad decisions have them facing this reality. Some of you have as well. They typically have one of two mindsets:

- *They have given up hope*, or

- *They know things have to change radically and quickly.*

Fortunately for Prodigal, his mind was fixed on the latter.

Even when fear of death leads or drives people to make the right decision to change, it may not happen quickly…or at all. Some people make decisions with good intentions to effect changes in their lives but fail to follow through on them. Failure to do so very often leads to severe consequences. The high recidivism rates for prisons and substance abuse treatment centers bear this out. At this point in Prodigal's story, the jury was still out.

Reality #3: True change begins deep in the heart

"I will set out and go to my father, and will say to him, 'Father, I have sinned against heaven, and in your sight; I am no longer worthy to be called your son; treat me as one of your hired laborers.'"

In the first chapter, we discussed Prodigal's state of mind and the condition of his heart. He was ambitious (no problem there) but also self-centered and inconsiderate and obviously discontent with the life and blessings he enjoyed.

That was then, and this is now, as the song goes. Jesus provided no timeline, so we have no idea how long it took for Prodigal to lose it all and hit rock bottom. But everything about his words and attitude in this passage demonstrated a dramatic change of heart. Let's take a closer look at four evidences of the changes in his heart that led to changes in his behavior.

Repentance

"...I will set out and go to my father..."

The Greek word for repentance is *metanoia*. One of the more prominent meanings is "to change one's mind or purpose for the better as a result of gaining knowledge." Other meanings include "turn and go the other way."

To say repentance is the most important message in the New Testament is not an overstatement. Forms of the word are used twenty-two times. The two most prominent were from John the Baptist and Jesus. In nearly identical words, both stated their missions as having come "to call sinners to repentance" (Matthew 3:2; 4:17).

Finally, after all that happened to Prodigal on his journey and having landed at rock bottom, he now had a *repentant heart*. He owned his sins. He decided things had to change, or he would die. He made the decision to turn around and go another way. This defines repentance. It is the one place everyone must find themselves at some point in their lives if they desire, above all, eternal life with God, found only through a relationship with Jesus Christ.

Confession

"Father, I have sinned against heaven and in your sight..."

That lonely place of repentance is very hard to come to. Once there, it does not get easier. The need for and practice of confession are found throughout Scripture. It is an admission, mentally and orally, that we have disobeyed God and fallen short or missed the mark, as the word *sin* is often defined. Prodigal confessed in his mind at this point. The oral version came later.

Following are two of my favorite Bible passages on confession. The first is the actual confession of King David in his most repentant state. He wrote this psalm after sins of adultery with Bathsheba and the murder of Uriah, her husband. The depths of David's despair can be felt in his words as he seeks God's forgiveness:

Be gracious to me, God, according to Your faithfulness; according to the greatness of Your compassion, wipe out my wrongdoings. Wash me thoroughly from my guilt and cleanse me from my sin. For I know my wrongdoings, and my sin is constantly before me. Against You, You only, I have sinned and done what is evil in Your sight...
Psalm 51:1-4

In the second example, the apostle John gave instructions to seekers and Christians who know they have sinned and need God's forgiveness:

"If we confess our sins, He is faithful and righteous to forgive us our sins and to cleanse us from all unrighteousness. If we say that we have not sinned, we make Him a liar and His word is not in us." 1 John 1:9-10

Prodigal recognized his sin was twofold. First, he sinned against God, and we know that all sin creates a break in our relationship with Him. Second, he sinned against his earthly father, whom he treated so disrespectfully.

Contrition

"I am no longer worthy to be called your son..."

The word *contrition* is used in some versions of the Bible but unfamiliar to many readers. I used it because it is a powerful word in this context. *Contrition* means *brokenness, a place of great sorrow and regret.*

In another of David's laments to the Lord, we find him in a place and posture that presents the best biblical example of contrition:

> *"The sacrifices of God are a broken spirit; a broken and contrite heart, God, you will not despise." Psalm 51:17*

Contrition goes deeper than repentance and confession to the point of having a broken heart and spirit. David poured out his feelings to the Lord: *deep, profound regret and sorrow*. It does not get any stronger than that.

Thus far, Prodigal verbalized to himself what he would say to his father. But actions speak louder than words. We need to know to what extent Prodigal was willing to go that would affirm the sincerity of his thought process. We have that in the final phrase.

Utter Humility

> *"...treat me as one of your hired laborers."*

Recall that Prodigal had been slopping hogs, the lowest job a Jew could have because swine were among the unclean animals in the sight of God. It was beyond humbling; it was humiliating.

Despite that, Prodigal was now willing to ask his father to send him to that same filthy place. Hired laborers did that kind of work, not sons. Prodigal knew he had forfeited his rights as a son through his sins: selfish demands and immature actions. He would not ask for reinstatement, just a place among the servants because they had it better than he did. He would no longer be part of the family, but at least he would not starve to death. More importantly, he might also have his father's forgiveness.

At the end of this part of Prodigal's story, we clearly see one of the lessons Jesus was trying to teach his audience: *the difference between dying and dying to self!*

Questions for Discussion

1) What were the three "new realities" that confronted Prodigal after he "came to his senses"?

a. _____

_____

_____

b. _____

_____

_____

c. _____

_____

_____

2) I identified two groups of people from the ways they respond to and deal with trouble and adversity in their lives. What were they?

a. _____

_____

_____

b. _____

_____

_____

Give an example or two of situations where you responded in one of those two ways.

_____

_____

_____

3) List the four words I used to make the case that Prodigal had a change of heart and describe a place or point in your life when you found yourself in a similar one.

a. _____

_____

_____

b. _____

_____

_____

c. _____

_____

_____

d. _____

_____

_____

CHAPTER EIGHT

That First Step Is Always the Hardest

"So he got up and went to his father…"
Luke 15:20, NIV

As the last chapter closed, Prodigal was making plans to return to his father and beg forgiveness. The words he rehearsed seemed convincing that his heart was finally in the right place. But up to that point, they were just that: *words*. He had yet to take that difficult first step.

We have a saying in the South that applies to putting our words into action: "Your talk walks." For Prodigal, that meant his repentant and contrite words would be nothing more than *failed good intentions* if he stayed away. For his "talk to walk," he had to return home and face his father and any consequences of his wasteful life abroad.

Early in the story, Jesus told us Prodigal left home and traveled to a far country. Assuming he remained in that general area during this season spent celebrating his *freedom*, the return trip would have been approximately the same distance. It also seems logical to think it would take about the same amount of time. Does that matter? It does in one sense.

Prodigal sons and daughters who traveled roads littered with bad decisions and rock-bottom outcomes learned the hard way that the distance home may have been the same, but the journey itself seemed excruciatingly longer. Why? *Tolls.* Every bad road we chose extracted a toll on our lives that wore us down, sometimes to the point of breaking.

Toll Roads of Life

Most people know toll roads are state or interstate highways that require a toll (payment) from the traveler. Many were built to provide a more expedient means of getting where they want to go. Other routes are available that take us to our destinations, but toll roads often provide a shortcut or easier way to our destination for which we are willing to pay.

As a product of the fall of Adam and Eve, mankind is forced to travel far more difficult roads through life than God intended. The perfect roads of Eden became rough and dangerous, fraught with steep hills, blind curves, and treacherous potholes. Some of them even lead us into dark places not on any map.

All of us have had times in our lives when things became unbearable to us. The prospect of finding an easier or shorter road out became very attractive. We were even willing to pay to remove the pain or gain our freedom.

I could make the case Prodigal did this by demanding his inheritance prematurely to placate his discontented heart. He never considered whether or not there would be a cost involved. Based on his attitude at the time, it would not have made any difference.

Later, Jesus described how the consequences of Prodigal's decision to "take the money and run" led to harsh, difficult roads that, over time, extracted tremendous tolls on his life. He was broke, starving to death, and stranded in a foreign land with no hope in sight.

There was one good thing about Prodigal's place: He had finally come to the end of his toll roads that drained him personally, materially, and spiritually. That only happens when we come to the end of ourselves. Now he was ready to take the hardest step of all: that first step home.

Most of us cannot directly relate to the specifics of Prodigal's life and journey as Jesus told his story. I do not know anyone who demanded his or her share of the family fortune (assuming there was one), ran off to parts unknown, blew it all partying, and ended up broke and humiliated. I am sure there are people like that. I just do not know any.

But many of us can relate to Prodigal's conditions once he arrived at the end of himself.

Broke. Broken. Exhausted. Empty.

As I considered his place and how he got there, it occurred to me that each condition had a corresponding *type* of toll associated with it that many of us have paid:

- Material (broke)

- Emotional (broken)

- Physical (exhausted)

- Spiritually (empty)

Examining these four types of tolls, in light of my own life and the lives of others I have known (or their stories), provided helpful insights into how each one has affected my life and relationship with my Father (God), then and now. I believe it can do the same for you.

Material Tolls

Prodigal lost his entire inheritance: *money and possessions*. He went from a position of plenty, with no material needs, to abject poverty. Prodigal paid the ultimate material toll; he was broke.

Perhaps you have been there or know someone whose lifestyle mirrored that of Prodigal's "riches to rags" story. I feel certain all of us can identify with bank balances that hovered at or below $0. Some of us even learned that banks have their own way of letting us know we are broke: NSF.

For those fortunate enough not to have ever been overdrawn, NSF is bank language for "insufficient funds." To make matters worse, the bank charges significant fees when you already don't have money to cover the check or debit charge that bounced! Oh, the irony!

The overarching issue for these material scenarios, from Prodigal's total loss to our overspending, is *stewardship*. Though He did not address that subject in this parable, Jesus taught a great deal on money. Obviously, *stewardship* was a term and concept unfamiliar to Prodigal. Sadly, the same can be said of many people, even those in the church.

Stewardship can be simply defined as "taking care of that which has been entrusted to you." Jesus told several parables with lessons about stewardship. Biblical stewardship is taking care of that which *God* entrusts to you and me. In church-speak, it is often referred to as the *three T's: treasure, talents*, and *time*. Good stewardship demands responsibility and calls for accountability.

But Satan, the deceiver, has the ability to make roads in front of us seem expedient or safe shortcuts when they are really fraught with potholes like *greed* and *excess*. Both are known to plunge people into untenable levels of *debt* that can take years to recover from. He makes other roads pleasing to the senses. They give the appearance of pleasure and the feel of a smooth ride but only lead us into dark places like *addiction* and *poverty*.

The best question I have found to encourage and challenge us to examine our stewardship and the material roads we choose is this:

> *Do you own your wealth and possessions, or do they own you?*

Jesus taught the following to His disciples in the Sermon on the Mount:

> *"No one can serve two masters; for either he will hate the one and love the other, or he will be devoted to one and despise the other. You cannot serve God and wealth." Matthew 6:24*

Emotional Tolls

We observed the devastating endpoints of Prodigal's bad decisions. Being broke was just the beginning. Much worse was the humbling that came from having to work as a hired hand, no longer a beloved son, now a paid servant. But it got worse. Prodigal went from being broke and humbled to utter humiliation when he was forced to work with pigs, an unclean animal, still considered as such today by many Jews.

When we fall that far in life, the ante gets higher. We go beyond the material toll and add what is referred to as an *emotional toll*. It affects our attitude, self-esteem, and clarity of thought. Emotional tolls often leave us in one of two places: *sinking deeper into despair* or *determined to find a way out*. Fortunately, Prodigal chose the latter.

What is the lesson for us? Despite the emotional tolls our journey through life extracts from us, like Prodigal, we still have a choice to make. *Give up or get up!*

Two verses from Scripture speak to this. The first is a well-known verse written by the apostle Paul:

> *"I can do all things through Him [Christ] who strengthens me." Philippians 4:13*

It is important to understand the context to extract the power from this verse. Paul wrote this letter to the church in Philippi from a Roman prison.

In addition to the strength he gained through Christ, Paul also shared that, despite the sufferings he encountered, he had learned the great lesson of *contentment*. Prodigal was learning this the hard way, like so many of us.

The second verse was written by the apostle John:

> *"For whoever has been born of God overcomes the world; and this is the victory that has overcome the world: our faith."* 1 John 5:4

Again, context is important. John was the last surviving apostle of Jesus. He was exiled to the island of Patmos for many years because of his faith and outspoken teachings of Jesus. He is said to have been in his nineties when he wrote his Gospel and the three epistles (letters) to the churches.

Despite all John endured, even seeing fellow apostles killed for their faith, he called Christians victorious overcomers. He reminded them that faith was the key to true successful living, as it remains today.

We also must learn to ask the Lord to increase our faith when Satan or life have extracted great emotional tolls from us, and we need strength to *get up, not give up.*

Physical Tolls

As if being broke (material tolls) and at his wit's end (emotional tolls) were not enough, Prodigal told us very plainly he was starving to death. He was severely undernourished, emotionally stressed from being forced to feed and tend pigs, and now engaged in hard physical labor, trying to survive. His bad decisions had also taken a physical toll on his life.

Fortunately, it would appear this incredibly unhealthy physical situation was the "straw that broke the camel's back" for Prodigal. From this place, we conclude he became determined and highly motivated to return home.

I confess that this section, more than any other, had me scratching my head about how to relate such extreme tolls on Prodigal's life to ours. I have ministered to many women and men over the years who, like Prodigal, found themselves *hungry, homeless*, and seemingly, *helpless*.

It was obvious they had paid great tolls along their journeys, including physical ones. There is a bedraggled look to their appearance. Their eyes often reflect the despair that permeates their lives.

Physical extremes of that nature do not often describe most of us. But that does not mean we do not pay physical tolls in our lives. Bad decisions of all kinds require tolls, regardless of our zip codes.

Physical tolls may result from emotional ones. Excessive stress is known to cripple people physically as well. Two of the best examples were the experiences of David that he shared in the psalms about times of emotional and physical distress.

On one occasion, surrounded by enemies who wanted to destroy him, David described the great fear that overwhelmed him:

"I am poured out like water, and all my bones are out of joint. My heart is like wax; it is melted within me. My strength is dried up like a piece of pottery, and my tongue clings to my jaws; and You lay me in the dust of death."Psalm 22:14-15

Have you ever been so scared you could not function physically? That is fear!

On another occasion, David was overwhelmed by the conviction of his great sin. To be more specific, his physical suffering came as a result of not confessing those sins. He wrote: "When I kept silent about my sin, my body wasted away through my groaning all day long. For day and night Your hand was heavy upon me; my vitality failed as with the dry heat of summer." Psalm 32:3-4

David learned the hard way of the emotional and physical consequences of sin when we fail to *come clean* before God. Let this be a reminder to us all!

Remember to Sabbath

Before I move on, let me say a few words about our physical need for *rest* to avoid paying those tolls. Americans, perhaps more than any other civilization, pay physical tolls for failing to "take care of our temples." That was part of the apostle Paul's admonition to the church in Corinth in these words:

"Do you not know that your bodies are temples of the Holy Spirit, who is in you, whom you have received from God? You are not your own; you were bought at a price. Therefore honor God with your bodies." 1 Corinthians 6:19-20

Some of us are borderline workaholics whose ideas of rest and relaxation can be more stressful than work. This is not what God intended. Even secular experts agree rest is critical to allowing our bodies and minds to heal and renew themselves.

That's why God gave Israel the Sabbath. On the first page of our Bible, we read God created everything in six days, but on the seventh day, *He rested* (Genesis 2:2-3). I am relatively certain He was not tired. He rested because He wanted to demonstrate to His created beings (us) the need for physical rest for our health and well-being. The Sabbath rest was created by God for His people to rest and focus on Him. It became one of the Ten Commandments.

One question remains: *If God took a day off to rest, shouldn't we?*

Spiritual Tolls

Prodigal had finally come to the end of himself. The sins of his lifestyle left him in the hardest place imaginable. But there was one toll yet to pay: *the spiritual toll.*

The good news is Prodigal was broken, contrite, and repentant for all his sins. From the time he disrespected his father and left with the inheritance until now, as he finally "limped" home to seek his father's forgiveness, Prodigal was ready to pay.

But payment of this toll would be different. This time Prodigal was willing to offer his repentance and his life in service to his father, hoping to receive forgiveness for his sins. His father alone could pardon them. He hoped for no more than that. Before we observe that encounter, let's consider the spiritual toll sin takes on our lives.

Like Prodigal, all of us must eventually pay the ultimate *spiritual toll* for the decisions we make and the roads we take. It is the most demanding toll of all: *our lives for our sins*. It is the **death** toll. No one can escape it no matter what we attempt or how hard we try.

Even those who claim to have lived *good* lives will find they were *not good enough,* as the apostle Paul explained in two critical verses:

- *"For all have sinned and fall short of the glory of God." Romans 3:23*

- *"For the wages of sin is death..." Romans 6:23*

The two keywords are highlighted so you do not miss them: *all* and *death*.

From Genesis 3 to the present, sin has been extracting *spiritual tolls* on all human lives. It plays no favorites,

115

demanding payment from people from all walks of life, regardless of who they are and where they live. Throughout our lives, these tolls take different forms with varying degrees of impact as they occur.

But at the end of our journeys, a demand for payment is made. It is the same toll for all, death! Again, the apostle Paul wrote:

> *"Indeed, we had the sentence of death within ourselves so that we would not trust in ourselves, but in God who raises the dead." 2 Corinthians 1:9*

Sadly, too many people begin their journey home full of themselves, unrepentant, and spiritually lost, just like Prodigal before he "came to his senses." They insist their way is best. They just want to have fun and enjoy life to the fullest. *Sin* is just another politically incorrect term used by judgmental Christians.

Prodigal was headed for a meeting with his father, who alone could forgive him. Taking that first step toward him was the hardest Prodigal had ever taken. He had no idea what his father would say or how he would respond.

All of us are also headed for a meeting with the Father, God, Who offers us forgiveness through Jesus Christ alone. His bloody, horrific death of crucifixion on the cross paid the final *spiritual toll* for the sins of all who come with repentant hearts and receive Him as Savior. The final jeopardy question for you is this:

Are you willing to take that first step toward Jesus or pay the final toll yourself?

Questions for Discussion

1) Before Prodigal took that first step toward home, I noted four conditions of his life that developed as a result of prodigal living. What were they?

    a. _____

    b. _____

    c. _____

    d. _____

2) Four types of *tolls* came as a result of his prodigal living and bad decisions. List each and, in the space below, add your story, similar or different things you may have experienced.

a. _____ Tolls

_____

_____

_____

b. _____ Tolls

_____

_____

_____

c. _____ Tolls

_____

_____

_____

d. _____ Tolls

_____

_____

_____

3) What was the final *spiritual toll?* Why must it be paid, and how?

_____

_____

_____

_____

_____

_____

CHAPTER NINE

An Unexpected Homecoming

But while he was still a long way off, his father saw him and felt compassion, and ran and embraced him and kissed him. And the son said to him, "Father, I have sinned against heaven and before you. I am no longer worthy to be called your son." But the father said to his servants, "Bring quickly the best robe, and put it on him, and put a ring on his hand, and shoes on his feet. And bring the fattened calf and kill it, and let us eat and celebrate. For this my son was dead, and is alive again; he was lost, and is found." And they began to celebrate. Luke 15:20-24, ESV

Prodigal struggled to keep putting one foot in front of the other; his father's house was now coming into view far off in the distance. Perhaps his eyes were playing tricks on him. After all, he was exhausted and starving. Against the setting sun, he saw the outline of a man who appeared to be running toward him. His first thought may have been he was in trouble and retribution approached. Had his prodigal ways finally caught up with him?

Prodigal left home a beloved son. His hope upon returning was that his father would at least receive him back as a servant. As the figure running toward him drew closer,

Prodigal rubbed his eyes in disbelief. It was his father. He had no idea why or what to expect when the two came together, once again face to face.

Much to Prodigal's amazement, his father recognized his bedraggled figure a long way from the house. He was so glad to see Prodigal that he did something considered very undignified for a Jewish father and landowner. *He pulled up his robe*, exposing his legs, so it would not get in the way. Then *the father ran* toward his younger son.

Why would the father do that? Prodigal was the long, lost son who left so rudely and abruptly. He may have been dead for all the father knew.

In God's eyes, the nation of Israel was a lot like Prodigal centuries before Jesus told this story. Israel was known for pridefully disobeying God and running away from Him. Yet He was always willing to forgive when the people repented and returned to Him. God kept His side of the covenant with Israel as demonstrated in these words from the prophet Malachi:

> *"From the days of your fathers you have turned aside from my statutes and have not kept them. Return to me, and I will return to you, says the LORD of hosts." Malachi 3:17, ESV*

Do not miss this important point that is too often mistaught. Running to Prodigal was the father's response to Prodigal's repentant heart and decision to return to him. Recall, from the beginning of the story, the father allowed Prodigal to leave and did not pursue him at any point in the story. That is consistent with God's words to His *children*, the nation of Israel.

This is the point in the story that Jesus began to teach His audience what a real loving father looked like and how he behaved toward his children, no matter what they had done. I sum it up this way: *The love of the father was stronger than the sins of his son. Love does not care what other people think.*

This father met his son where he was: *broken*, *contrite*, and *exhausted*. Instead of greeting Prodigal with scorn and rebuke, he ran to Prodigal and began to hug and kiss him. Not a word of rebuke or judgment. Just glad to see him alive again.

As his father embraced him, Prodigal began to repent and offered his broken-hearted confession. Before getting through all he planned to say, his father cut him off, quick to forgive his wayward son.

He ordered the servants to clothe Prodigal with a robe. He told them to put a ring on his finger. He added shoes for Prodigal's cut, bruised, and weary feet. Finally, Prodigal's father ordered the fattened calf killed and a party to be held to honor Prodigal's return. The son, who lost his way when he forsook everyone and everything, found his way back to his father's loving arms.

Now it is your turn to take center stage and replace Prodigal as this part of the story unfolds with his inglorious, not so triumphant return. Let's consider the sequence of events as they played out for Prodigal and how they relate to your story.

Remembering

If you are a parent, it is not surprising to us that the father looked up and recognized his weary son while he was still a long distance away after an extended absence. We do not know the length of that absence. Perhaps it was long enough that Prodigal had some concern over whether or not his father would recognize or even remember him. You have to be in a very bad state of mind or away for a very long time to think your parents would not remember you.

I have good news for you. In the same way Prodigal's father remembered his son, God our Father never forgets you, no matter what you have done or how long you have been estranged from Him. You are never out of His sight and never unloved! I have used these verses in Isaiah many times to encourage homeless or imprisoned men and women:

> But Zion said, "The LORD has abandoned me and the Lord has forgotten me." "Can a woman forget her nursing child and have no compassion on the son of her womb? Even these may forget, but I will not forget you. Behold, I have inscribed you on the palms of My hands; Your walls are continually before Me." Isaiah 49:14-16

When I teach that passage, I love to ask men and women to look at their lifelines, the creases in the palms of their hands. Then I tell them to imagine that one of those lines represents his or her life inscribed on the palm of God's hand. It is a great visual and reminder that God never forgets you or me. He has inscribed us on the palms of His hands.

Repentance

Keep in mind that Prodigal returned home a broken, humbled young man who began to repent and seek forgiveness as soon as he was in his father's presence.

> *"Father, I have sinned against heaven and in your sight; I am no longer worthy to be called your son." Luke 15:21*

He could not wait to get those words out of his mouth. That bore evidence Prodigal really had repented of his sins, wanted to confess them, and sought his father's forgiveness.

People who are truly repentant not only feel it in their hearts, but they also confess their sins. Jesus told us His mission on earth was simple: *He came to call sinners to repentance.* That includes you and me. Prodigal repented and confessed his sin to his father, and so must we. Only then can we expect to receive the greatest news of all…

Forgiveness

Prodigal had not finished saying all his repentant heart had prepared before his father forgave him and moved on. God does the same when we confess our sins. The apostle John wrote:

> *"If we confess our sins, He is faithful and righteous, so that He will forgive us our sins and cleanse us from all unrighteousness." 1 John 1:9*

There is another wonderful aspect to the forgiveness of God. It is always accompanied by His *forgetfulness*. God does not have a bad memory. He just promised that if we could receive His forgiveness through Christ, He would forget our sins. We take great comfort from the words of the prophet Jeremiah:

> *"... for I will forgive their wrongdoing, and their*
> *sin I will no longer remember." Jeremiah 31:34*

The challenge most of us face is learning to forgive ourselves and put our sins in the past. Joy returns to life when we get on the other side of that.

Restoration

As soon as Prodigal confessed and received the forgiveness of his father, Jesus told us the father did not dwell on the past. He proceeded immediately to the wonderful process of *restoring* his beleaguered son back into the family. Each gift, the robe, the ring, and the sandals represented a step in that process:

- The robe was a sign of forgiveness and restoration— put off the old and filthy garments for a new clean robe.

- The ring was given to special guests of honor when they came to someone's home. It was also a symbol of dignity and authority.

- The sandals may have meant the most to Prodigal. Servants did not wear them. Sons and daughters did. This was the sign that Prodigal would not have to work as a servant in his father's fields, though his humbled heart was willing to.

Each of us is treated in the same manner when we come to our Heavenly Father as Prodigal did his.

Celebration

The culminating act was one of honoring Prodigal upon his return. His father ordered the best veal on the farm (the fatted calf) killed and made ready for a feast to celebrate his homecoming. Such a celebration was reserved for special, honored guests.

Two things to know about your homecoming celebration. If you are born again in Christ, at the moment of your conversion, there was a great celebration in Heaven. Jesus said:

> "...there is joy in the presence of the angels of God over one sinner who repents." Luke 15:10

The second celebration comes after we are finally Home with the Lord. It is often called the wedding feast and described in the Book of Revelation. It signifies the consummation of the marriage of Jesus the Bridegroom to His beautiful church. That means those of us who are born-again in Christ. We are His bride. This will be the greatest feast of all, held in our honor:

> "Then he [the angel of the Lord] said to me [John the apostle], 'Write: "Blessed are those who are

127

invited to the wedding feast of the Lamb."'"
Revelation 19:9

Your blood-stained invitation to the celebration awaits at the foot of the Cross of Christ!

Questions for Discussion

Reflect on the five parts to the story of Prodigal's homecoming. Note any similarities with your story, and please, add anything that fits yours but may not have been part of his. There are no right or wrong answers; just write what the Holy Spirit brings to mind when you consider your life in light of each part of Prodigal's return.

Remembering

_____

_____

_____

Repentance

_____

_____

_____

Forgiveness

_____

_____

_____

Restoration

_____

_____

_____

Celebration

_____

_____

_____

CHAPTER TEN

Not Everyone Is Glad You're Home

Now his older son was in the field, and when he came and approached the house, he heard music and dancing. And he summoned one of the servants and began inquiring what these things could be. And he said to him, "Your brother has come, and your father has killed the fattened calf because he has received him back safe and sound." But he became angry and was not willing to go in; and his father came out and began pleading with him. But he answered and said to his father, "Look! For so many years I have been serving you and I have never neglected a command of yours; and yet you have never given me a young goat, so that I might celebrate with my friends; but when this son of yours came, who has devoured your wealth with prostitutes, you killed the fattened calf for him." Luke 15:25-30

Jealousy has been referred to as "the green-eyed monster." The phrase was coined by the character Iago in Shakespeare's play *Othello* (1604). Everyone reading this book can identify with Shakespeare's metaphor and share personal examples in which jealousy overtook our emotions.

The objects of our jealousy are numerous. What is most interesting about them to me is that those objects are not objects at all, but people. I do not get jealous of things. I am jealous of the person that owns or possesses that thing. I am not jealous of your nicer car or larger home. I am jealous that you have them and not me.

Moral lessons on jealousy have filled the small and big screens for years. They range from old television shows like Andy Griffith teaching Opie such lessons to the movie classic, *Gone with the Wind*, in which Scarlett was the true "green-eyed monster" because Melanie was married to Ashley instead of her.

The truth is this "monster" has plagued men and women since our beginning. In Genesis, we read that Cain killed Abel because he was jealous and resentful that God received Abel's offering and not his. Thus, jealousy was the first motive for the first murder in the Bible.

There are many stories in the Bible in which the sin of jealousy reared its ugly head. One of the best that provides a great segue back to our story also involves a father and his sons. The issue was jealousy between brothers, specifically ten brothers against one. It is the story of Joseph that began to unfold in Genesis 37. Following is a summary of his story and the role jealously played.

Jacob was the son of Isaac, the son of Abraham, father of the nation of Israel. Jacob had twelve sons that would become the heads of the twelve tribes of Israel. Their stories and heritage follow throughout the entire Bible, even into the Revelation. But this story is on the front end of their lives.

Now Israel [Jacob] lovedJoseph more than all his other sons, because he was the son of his old age; and he made him a multicolored tunic. And his brothers saw that their father loved him more than all his brothers; and so they hated him and could not speak to him on friendly terms.

Genesis 37:3-4

Joseph was a "daddy's boy" and a tattletale (v2). Thus, his brothers hated and were very jealous of him. He even had a dream that one day his brothers would bow down to him. Unfortunately, he shared that with them, which was a big mistake. Their jealousy overtook any common sense, and they decided to kill him.

Reuben, the oldest brother, spoke against this. They decided to throw him into a pit instead and later sold him into slavery. Worst of all, they faked his death and told Jacob that his favorite son had been killed by wild animals. Joseph ended up as a slave in Egypt. The rest of his story is a long one that occupies the rest of the book of Genesis.

If you were a Sunday School kid who learned many of the famous Bible stories, you know that Joseph ultimately became ruler over all of Egypt, second only to the Pharaoh himself. Before this story ended, these brothers would, in fact, bow before their younger brother, whose vision years before made them so jealous of him; rather their father's love for him. Like so many of us who have felt slighted or overlooked, they must have asked among themselves, "What about us?" That question will soon resurface as our story continues.

****

This book could have ended with the previous chapter because Prodigal, our main character to this point, was safely home and restored to his father. But Jesus did not end the story with verse twenty-four. Why not? Everyone was happy, right? Not quite.

Early in the book, I mentioned that the most important thing to keep in context throughout Jesus' story is the audience. Two groups comprised the crowd that day: *lost sinners* and *self-righteous religious people*.

Prodigal represented the lost sinners. His sad and, at times, horrific story ended well. He repented and returned to his father, who restored him as a son.

But Jesus had only addressed part of His audience. Now He shifted the focus of the story to the self-righteous religious people. He did this indirectly by introducing the next character in the story: the older brother.

What About Me?

Before we begin discussing the older brother, I want to share a couple of thoughts to keep in mind. It is true that Prodigal, not his older brother, asked for his share of the inheritance. However, Jesus' words in verse twelve, *"he divided his wealth between them,"* let us know the entire inheritance was divided according to Jewish law. Thus, the older brother received or gained access to his rightful *double* portion.

Coming home from working his father's fields one day, the older brother heard music and became curious about what was going on at his father's house. A servant told him his younger brother had come home, and there was a big party in progress to celebrate. Most of us would think the older brother became excited that his little brother was safely home, right? Wrong!

Instead of joining the party and welcoming his little brother home, the older brother was very angry. In fact, he blatantly refused to join the party, despite his father's pleas. He went off, not on a journey, but into a tirade something like this:

I have been the dutiful son who stayed in his rightful place.

I obeyed everything you told me to do.

You never gave me anything, not even a goat, to party with my friends.

You caved in to the selfish demand of your younger son.

He squandered all of it with prostitutes (a great sin for Jewish men).

After all that, when "this son of yours" returned, you honored him.

You expect me to join a party to welcome him back?

Indeed, after all that, why should the older brother join the celebration of the return of a worthless, disobedient son who wasted his father's wealth on prostitutes of all people?

To many of us, the older brother's anger seemed justified. Everything he said was true. What was wrong with his attitude? To answer what seems to be a fair question, let's remember Jesus was the storyteller and teacher. His teachings always have life lessons, obvious and veiled. The father represents God.

Following are the teachings (lessons) Jesus intended for His audience concerning the older son and his part of the conversation with his father. From that brief exchange, we learn a few things about his *attitude, words,* and *actions* toward his father, himself, and Prodigal.

Attitude Toward His Father

"Look!" That first word said all we needed to know to give us a peek into the heart of the older brother. Throughout the generations of biblical history, as in my own upbringing, speaking to your father with such a disrespectful tone of voice, at a minimum, would have seen him turn and walk away and, at worst, drawn a slap across the face.

Fathers were the most highly regarded members of a family, whether they deserved it or not. Typically, such conversations would begin by addressing him as *father*. If you recall, even Prodigal called him "father" before he made his demand and upon his return.

For the older son to have begun this conversation with such an abrupt demand could not have been more disrespectful. It was as if the older son was crying out, "What about me?"

His Own Attitude

The first revelation of the older son's character was on display *before* this conversation with his father. Recall that when he heard all the noise from the house as he came home from working, he did not inquire at all about Prodigal when told of his return.

Then we read the most obvious indicators of someone "full of self." He used the word "I" three times in one sentence. Throw in one "me" and another "my," and we have someone concerned only about himself. There was a sense of entitlement in what and how the older brother said things.

You have heard the expression, "It is not what you say but how you say it." There is some truth in that, even in this case. What the older brother said was true, but the manner in which he accosted his father and criticized Prodigal was also self-righteous and uncaring.

Though he never asked it out loud, the older brother's attitude, words, and actions silently shouted the question, "Why not me?"

His Attitude Toward Prodigal

The older brother showed ultimate disrespect when he would not refer to Prodigal as his brother. Rather, he referred to him as "this son of yours." All present that day would have agreed there was not a greater sign of disrespect between siblings than for one to refuse to recognize another as a sister or brother.

Throughout the Bible, from Adam and Eve to New Testament families, including that of Jesus, families were the backbone of societal life, godly and pagan. Relationships mattered. That was true for both groups in Jesus' audience. The Jewish leaders, so vigilant in knowing the Law even if they did not follow it, were keenly aware of this. They knew Jesus was referring to them!

Beyond the spoken disrespect, we hear hatefulness and resentment in his voice over what the father had *not* done for him and what he had done to celebrate Prodigal's return. There was a sense of self-righteous indignation and judgment toward Prodigal's sin when the older brother pointed out how he squandered his wealth.

The older brother may have thought to himself, *Prodigal got what he deserved by taking your money and running off like that, squandering all of it on prostitutes and God knows what else!*

After making himself out to be so righteous a son and pointing to the sin of Prodigal, I can imagine a new question raged in the heart of the older brother: *What about him?* as he pointed a blaming finger of condemnation in the direction of his younger brother.

It is worth noting that since the older brother refused to join the celebration, he could not witness for himself the brokenness and repentance of his younger brother. Instead, he chose to stand in judgment of Prodigal, maintaining an attitude of complete unforgiveness.

It is also noteworthy that despite the older son's rant toward his father and Prodigal, his father did not walk away or strike him for being disrespectful. Instead, he hung in there and listened quietly to all his disgusted older son had to say.

We will read how the father responded in the final chapter. But before going there, let's do some introspection of our own *attitudes, words,* and *actions* when we feel slighted or overlooked, when we ask our own version of the question, *"What about me?"*

Questions for Discussion

In this section of Scripture, Jesus focused on the older brother to teach the Pharisees and other religious Jews in His audience. If we are honest, there is *"Pharisee"* or *self-righteousness* in all of us, given the right circumstances. Consider these words used to describe the older brother, then write how each has described you and under what circumstances.

1) Disrespectful. Do your words communicate disrespect toward people who think differently than you or do not agree with your beliefs or values? If not words, can it be felt or seen in your attitudes?

_____

_____

_____

2) Resentment. Do you tend to resent people who get more than you or more than you think they deserve? Are you holding onto resentment against anyone in your life? Why?

_____

_____

_____

3) Self-righteousness. This is often more perceived by others than recognized by ourselves. Did Prodigal get what he

deserved? Do you consider the sins of others worse than yours? Do you judge people by your own values and beliefs or on your scale of what seems fair to you? (Trick question; we are not to judge people at all. But we do, so answer honestly.)

_____

_____

_____

4) Unforgiveness. Are there people in your life who have sinned against you or hurt you in some way to the point that you continue to hold a grudge or feel you cannot forgive them?

_____

_____

_____

CHAPTER ELEVEN

The Final Confrontation

"And he said to him, 'Son, you have always been with me, and all that is mine is yours. But we had to celebrate and rejoice because this brother of yours was dead and has begun to live, and was lost and has been found.'"

Luke 15:31-32

In the beautiful bluegrass state of Kentucky lived a man who bred and raised thoroughbred horses. The man had two sons that worked it with him who were very different in their styles and temperaments. One son was more laid back and easy-going, the other more direct and serious. They viewed the world in very different ways.

A new foal was born on the farm. He was born of championship stock. It was the practice of the father to have his sons take turns with the primary care and raising of each new colt. That would be a more difficult assignment with this one.

Almost as soon as the new colt could walk, he began getting into mischief. As soon as he learned to run, the owners knew they either had a potentially great racehorse or one more like a wild stallion. The question became whether or not they could tame this young colt and get him to accept the bit and bridle.

It seemed almost a contradiction that the easy-going son was tasked with raising this wild colt. They had completely opposite personalities. But the son loved this colt more than the others, despite the colt's wild and rebellious ways. His brother insisted the colt needed more discipline and stricter training. He was prone to use the whip rather than whispers.

Every chance the colt had, he took off. Many hours were spent chasing him down, trying to corral him. Then one night, the colt escaped from the barn and somehow managed to get completely off the farm into hundreds of wooded acres that surrounded the farm.

Days were spent searching for the colt to no avail. Eventually, the father called off the search despite the pleas of his son. He really had no choice because the search had turned up no sign of the colt, and there were other horses to be cared for and trained and limited resources for both people and money.

The son responsible for raising and caring for the colt grieved in his heart. He knew it was possible the horse might one day return to the farm, but even his hopes waned as weeks then months passed. The energetic, wild, young colt had found the freedom he wanted, but at what cost?

One night, months after all hope of finding the colt was lost, the father and sons were awakened by a great disturbance in and around the horse barn. They quickly threw on some clothes and grabbed their guns as they went out to investigate. To their amazement, they saw the long-lost colt pawing at the barn door and trying to push it open with his nose. He had never looked or acted so tame.

As they approached the colt, it became apparent he had been wounded. Dried blood was found in multiple places, evidence of attacks from wilder animals. They also noticed one other thing that is often fatal for racehorses.

To keep him from running off again, they quickly put a halter on him. They soon discovered that was not necessary. The colt limped badly when they tried to walk him. It was painfully evident that one of his legs was damaged; how much they would not know until the vet x-rayed it.

Then the bad news came. The colt had a leg fracture that would keep it from ever racing. The horse could live with the fracture, but was it worth the investment of time and money to keep him alive if he could never race? Horse farms can run in the "red" during the dry years between "winners." But that is not sustainable. A life or death decision had to be made, and it fell on the father.

The sons weighed in. The pragmatic older son declared the colt, wild from its birth, should be put down because he could not ever race and would be a financial burden to the farm. Besides, none of this would have happened to him if he had not run away.

The son who cared for the colt and felt his loss the most held the opposite opinion. But his argument was mostly based on feelings, not facts. The father had a decision to make: *Put the colt down* or *let him live*, hoping one day he could be put to stud.

The father understood even better than his sons the weight of the financial burden the injured colt would place on the farm. But compassion won out over currency, and the father agreed to keep the colt and raise him with the others. That turned out to be a good decision.

I noted at the beginning of the story the colt was born of championship bloodlines. Just because the horse never raced and had a cracked bone in his leg did not prevent him from siring other colts. The last foal became a champion, returning many-fold the time and money invested in his father—the wild one who could not be tamed and was "not worth the trouble."

****

As we read in the last chapter, sibling rivalries are well-known between kids in the same family, regardless of age and period in history. One child resents another or becomes jealous when a sibling receives more than he or she thinks is fair. Life lessons on *fairness* are some of the more difficult ones to teach and learn.

From that sense of *fairness* came the thought process that people should get what they deserve based on their actions, good and bad. We noted a "got what he deserved" mindset oozing through the cracks in the self-righteous older brother's hard heart. As we study the last two verses in this story, we will see how Jesus addressed both *fairness* and *get what you deserve* in the way He told us how the father responded to the older brother.

As we begin the final part of the story, the older brother had just finished a strong, self-righteous rant against Prodigal and his father. There were elements of truth in everything he said. After patiently listening, the father finally weighed in on all that had transpired up to that point, from the time the younger son demanded his inheritance and left until his return and the party that was now in progress to celebrate it.

Despite the disrespectful attitude and language of his older son, the father began by affirming him. The older son had, indeed, been faithful to remain with his father and did the work that was expected of him. One thing stood out to me about what may have been the expectations of the older brother. Most of us would agree we do not typically throw parties or celebrate someone for doing what is expected. "Participation trophies" did not exist in Jesus' day!

The father certainly could have challenged the older son about the motive and condition of his own heart. Instead, *the heart of the father was as patient toward his older son as it was compassionate toward the younger. Love for both was obvious.*

The second part of the father's affirmation acknowledged the position and inheritance of his oldest son. Recall that the inheritance had already been divided between the sons. If it had not been physically distributed to him, it was available for whatever purpose he chose whenever he wanted it, including partying with his friends.

So the older son had no valid reason to complain about anything his younger brother did or that his return was being celebrated. Prodigal's disrespect, defiance, and disobedience were between him and their father. This would be like your older brother or sister complaining because your parents did not spank or ground you for something he or she thought you deserved. Some of us probably did that.

The truth of that matter was the older brother had no role or part in the process, affirming or disciplinary. It was *his choice* to rant, complain, and stay away.

The Big Picture from the Father's View

As I mentioned previously, Jesus told two other parables in Luke 15 that led up to this story. The first concerned a lost sheep; the second a lost coin. Both stories end with key verses similar to verse thirty-two in this passage. They speak to how the person who lost something responded upon finding that which was lost. In both parables, the reactions were the same, *rejoicing* and *celebration*.

At the end of the lost sheep story, Jesus said to the crowd:

> *"I tell you that in the same way, there will be more joy in heaven over one sinner who repents than over ninety-nine righteous persons who need no repentance." Luke 15:7*

And in very similar words at the end of the lost coin story, Jesus also said,

> *"I tell you that in the same way, there will be more joy in heaven over one sinner who repents than over ninety-nine righteous persons who need no repentance." Luke 15:10*

Jesus equated both *lost-found* scenarios with *sinners who repented.*

For the father, there was no decision to make. Celebration was not just called for; the situation demanded it! Prodigal had returned to seek forgiveness, and his father gave it to him. Party time!

To close this parable, Jesus offered two compelling analogies to describe how the father viewed the return, redemption, and restoration of Prodigal. He hoped it would help his oldest understand and finally agree to join the party. In the first part of the verse, he said:

> "...this brother of yours was dead and has be-
> gun to live."

There is much to unpack theologically and practically in these words. The father used the word *brother* to keep in front of his older son that the two were related by blood. Recall that the older had just referred to his brother as "*this son of yours*." Whether or not the older brother liked Prodigal did not matter; they were brothers. That gave the older brother a lot of heartburn because he obviously felt nothing but disdain and contempt for his younger sibling.

The Greek word for dead is *nekros*. It can mean literally *dead* as in *life has expired*; the *person that was is now a corpse*. It also means (as the Amplified Bible reads) *as good as dead*. Prodigal was obviously never dead in the literal sense. But he was *dead* to his father because he did not know where Prodigal was. As far as the father knew, Prodigal could have died or been killed.

When the younger son appeared on the horizon that day, the father was overcome with joy (and probably relief) to see his prodigal again. As far as he knew, this son was *dead*. Now he had come back to life. He had been *born again* in one sense.

The father continued his description of how he viewed the return of his younger son:

"...was lost and has been found."

I always felt that one of the key overlooked points to this story of redemption was *the father never made any efforts to find his son.* He waited on Prodigal to come home before running out to greet him. Now the lost son was found!

Everything about this amazing parable Jesus told that day resonated with His audience. The tax collectors and other sinners knew they were on center stage in the person of the wasteful, rebellious son who was lost to his father. Jesus was calling them to repent and come home—*get found.*

As the Pharisees listened, they knew their roles shifted from co-stars waiting in the wings of the story to center stage as this confrontation between the older son and father took place. They were exposed as an unloving and uncaring older brother, resentful of the father's forgiveness and acceptance of the sinful younger brother into the family.

Just as the father begged the older son to join the celebration, Jesus bid them to return to the family of God that celebrates all who repent and are born again by His blood. We know most Pharisees never accepted His offer. Rather they continued to cause trouble for Jesus and eventually succeeded in having Him put to death.

Sadly, when the story ended, the older brother had neither relented nor joined the party.

Questions for Discussion

The father finally took center stage in the closing section of Jesus' story. We know how he responded to the attitudes and actions of Prodigal. We also know how he spoke to his older son, whose true character was exposed when Prodigal returned a repentant, broken man seeking forgiveness.

1) The Father and the Prodigal Son. Write your thoughts on how the father handled this situation and note anything you may have added or done differently.

_____

_____

_____

2) The Father and the Older Brother. Now write your thoughts on how the father handled this situation and note anything you may have added or done differently.

_____

_____

_____

3) The story ended with the older brother still on the outside of the celebration, refusing to go inside. Why do you think Jesus ended the story that way?

_____

_____

_____

CHAPTER TWELVE

Saving Ret Law

We left Ret Law sitting alone in an apartment with a lot of questions, especially about God. Kids "raised in church" often find themselves at a place like this early in their adult lives. They come to a crossroads that requires a decision about what they really believe and the direction their lives will take based on those beliefs. It is time to separate parents' faith from their own, assuming any remains at this point.

There is an old saying in church circles, "*God does not have any grandchildren, just children.*" Young adults like Ret Law usually choose one of two paths:

God does not seem real; they don't like all the harsh things He does in the Bible and all its contradictions. Jesus can't be the only way to God. So they decide to stay where they are or walk further away.

OR

Their feelings are more than that. They cannot shake them. The conviction of the Holy Spirit in their lives remains strong, strong enough that they sense it is the real God calling. They decide to seek after Him no matter what or how long it takes.

Ret Law decided on the latter path. A friend from work invited him to attend church with his family. He thought that beat working on Sunday, and he could use a break.

he people at the church were friendly enough. The first thing he noticed was the preacher wore a robe, as did the choir. This looked pretty formal to him, so he prepared for what he thought would be a boring service.

He was blown away by the demeanor of the preacher and the way he talked about the *grace of God*. Ret Law did not know much about grace. This message was refreshing. Something "clicked" in his spirit, and church quickly became an important part of his life. This time it was his decision to go.

This is where salvation began for Ret Law. The strength of biblical teaching from his childhood brought verses back to mind as he wrestled through what he heard now and what he already knew. He knew a lot *about* God.

The nagging question that had gnawed at him for years was now front and center. *Had he really been born again* the way Jesus described to Nicodemus that night? It demanded an *honest* answer.

Ret Law knew well that verse in which Jesus explained to Nicodemus how a person was restored to God:

> *"Jesus responded and said to him, 'Truly, truly, I say to you, unless someone is born again he can-not see the kingdom of God.'" John 3:3*

In one of Apostle Paul's letters to the Corinthian church, he wrote perhaps the most powerful verse in the Bible that helps people examine their hearts to see if they really did receive

Christ and were born again in Him—*that critical move from knowing about Jesus to knowing Him*!

> *"Godly sorrow brings repentance that leads to salvation and leaves no regret, but worldly sorrow brings death."* 2 Corinthians 7:10, NIV

Like Prodigal, Ret Law finally experienced that godly sorrow and came to his senses. He knew, once and for all time, he was born again. A new story was beginning because a new life had begun.

Ret Law would be the first to tell you that this new life in Christ is a journey with three steps forward and two back, sometimes none forward and three back. There is an old football description one noted commentator used that applies well here: *"Rumbling, stumbling, bumbling."* The point is that we keep growing in the right direction!

Ret Law jumped in headfirst. Bible reading went from almost never to daily. Over time, studying replaced reading. Reading books by great Christian authors like Chuck Swindoll and Warren Wiersbe helped him grow tremendously in his walk with the Lord. Perhaps the most significant event was joining a Christian men's group and being discipled by an older Christian man, a spiritual father. The "fix" was in!

Ret Law's story is one of redemption and hope fulfilled. In some ways, his story parallels Prodigal's. Remembering that *prodigal* means *extravagantly wasteful,* he qualified. Realizing Jesus told two stories about things that were lost before He told the most personal one about *a son who was lost*; again, he qualified.

The story of Ret Law is true to the extent he could remember these events from four decades earlier. His name was not "changed to protect the innocent," as the old Dragnet TV show used to say about the characters.

Rather I did, what seemed to me at the time, a clever thing. I simply wrote his name backward—just his first name. That's right. The testimony of *Ret Law* is really that of *Walter*, me, your humble *formerly* prodigal and lost author.

I could not close the book without disclosing that and sharing a little more of my testimony about the love, grace, mercy, anger, discipline, and all the other attributes of God that affected my life before I came to salvation through Christ and since that time.

I went from sitting in an apartment feeling lonely and questioning God to my life today, blessed with a great wife and family, including two grandsons, caring Christian brothers and sisters, and a fulfilling career made even better as I finish my life *"doing the work of an evangelist and disciple-maker."*

My story will continue until one of two things happens: *The Lord takes me home* (meaning I go to sleep in the Lord aka death), or *the rapture of His church occurs where we meet Jesus in the clouds and are whisked on to Heaven!*

Now it is your turn. What about you? What is your story? I hope you were diligent to answer the questions provided to stimulate your thinking about areas in life that mirrored Prodigal's and his older brother. The good news is that, on the other side of your salvation, God has a purpose and plan for your life no matter where you are today!

At times in our lives, we have all been *wasteful* with what God has entrusted to us. And we have all been *lost* at some point...in need of a Savior. If that is where you are today, I wrote one more page for you to read. Please do not close this book before doing so.

For Christ's sake and yours,

Walter

Alias Ret Law

The Invitation

We finally arrived at the end of Prodigal's journey. On the front end, we saw a young man who bore some of the same negative characteristics many of us have in our lives: *rebellious, selfish, foolish.* We also suffered the consequences, perhaps finding ourselves *humiliated* and *sitting on rock bottom.*

All of that happened to bring Prodigal to one point: *a crisis of decision.* Humbled and broken, he made the decision to return home to his father, not knowing what to expect and willing to suffer any consequences.

This book was written to help you see yourself in any and every way possible through the life of Prodigal:

- Your selfish attitudes

- Your foolish decisions and consequences suffered

- What it took to bring you to your senses

As it did with Prodigal, all that serves one purpose: to bring us to *a crisis of decision.* It is not enough just to *come to our senses* and admit we have bottomed out. That is the right start, but if we do nothing more, we remain hopeless. We must also *decide* it is time to *get up and return* to our Father, seeking His forgiveness and help. He never refuses!

The father in Jesus' story represents God. Through the life of Prodigal and the response of his father, we learned much about the love of God and how He responds to rebellious sinners. That includes you and me.

The key lesson for us as sinners comes from what Prodigal did when *he came to his senses* and how the father received him when he got home. Prodigal was broken, contrite, and repentant; emphasis on *repentant.*

The father responded with amazing love, grace, mercy, and forgiveness. That is how God becomes our spiritual Father through Jesus Christ. We come with repentant hearts, broken over our sins and asking forgiveness. That kind of heart is met by God our Father in the same way Prodigal was met.

Prodigal *came to his senses* and recognized he was a sinner who needed to go to his father and ask forgiveness. All of us were in that place before we received Christ. The Holy Spirit leads you, as it did all who are in Christ, to the most important decision you will ever make in your life. And you will make it one way or the other, intentionally or by default.

My final words are to invite you to receive Christ as your Savior today. I cannot think of a better way to close this book than to share four key verses that will change your life forever *if* you understand and take them to heart.

Jesus' Invitation

> *"Come to Me, all who are weary and burdened, and I will give you rest. Take My yoke upon you and learn from Me, for I am gentle and humble in heart, and you will find rest for your souls. For*

My yoke is comfortable, and My burden is light."
Matthew 11:28-30

Answering *Why*?

"...for all have sinned and fall short of the glory of God..." Romans 3:23

Answering *How*?

"If we confess our sins, He is faithful and righteous, so that He will forgive us our sins and cleanse us from all unrighteousness." 1 John 1:9

Answering *What*?

"But as many as received Him, to them He gave the right to become children of God, to those who believe in His name." John 1:12

Welcome to the family of God! You are now a daughter or son of God Most High—a joint heir with Jesus Christ our Savior. In Heaven, angels are celebrating because another lost sinner has repented and received Jesus as Savior. We read that three times in Luke 15.

You brought to life the title of this book, and God answered my prayer that you would meet Him here and say yes! My prayer now is that you allow the Holy Spirit to work on, in, and through you to make Him Lord of your life as you grow up in Christ.

To God be the glory, great things He has done! Amen.

Other Resources from Walter Spires

Hundreds of Walter's lessons and messages are available in three formats for your convenience: video, audio, written. You can find them here:

YouTube Channel: OnlyJesusLife

Website: www.onlyjesus.life

Podcast: www.anchor.fm/onlyjesus

Website: www.desperatemen.org

Podcast: www.anchor.fm/walter-spires

Print and eBooks

All Men Are Desperate Whether They Admit It or Not, Ingram-Spark Publishing, 2016, ISBN 978-0-9977185-0-8 (Print); 978-0-9977185-1-5 (e-book)

How the Christian Church in America Is Failing Men, e-booklet with videos, 2018

Power Tools – Build People Who Succeed in Life, Kendall-Hunt Publishing, 1995, ISBN 0-7872-0588-5

Social Media

Facebook

www.facebook.com/onlyjesus.life

www.facebook.com/questionsforgod.me

Twitter

Walter@OnlyJesu1

Walter@DesperateMen2

Instagram

Walterspiresonlyjesus

desperatemenorg

About the Author—Walter Spires

"Teaching biblical truth with passion and compassion"

"I love studying and teaching the Word of God with the integrity in which it was written to equip, encourage, and exhort men and women from all walks of life, regardless of zip code, to find the love of God poured out for all sinners through Jesus Christ, our only hope for salvation."

For more than twenty years, Walter has been evangelizing and discipling men and women in places most hope they never find themselves: rescue missions, life recovery programs, and prison. His mission field also includes places where people are more easily found and often just as needy, the church.

Prior to God's call, Walter spent most of his professional career in corporate healthcare leadership roles. He was part of several start-up ventures and later started an advisory company focused on developing servant-leaders, high-performance people, and teams.

Walter is the author of three published books and one e-book. He was a motivational speaker, equipping and encouraging thousands of people at corporate, association, and ministry events. He hosted a radio program called *Minute for Men* and has been a guest on radio and television.

alter and Gigi have been married thirty-eight years and reside in Franklin, Tennessee. They have three grown children, two of whom are married, and two amazing grandsons.